I0842977

INTO THE HINTERLANDS

BEYOND SECOND COGNITION

BY

ENDALL BEALL

Dedication

This book is dedicated to the generations of the future who will benefit the most from this work.

Table of Contents

Acknowledgements

I would like to acknowledge my editors and all those who have supported us and benefitted from our work over the past few years. You all know who you are.

Foreword

I began my PSOYCA work a few years ago. After reading several of Endall's books I knew this was my path and that I would set about to accomplish the goal of cognitive advancement up to and including second cognition and beyond.

I had been driven most of my life to seek answers about the nature of our reality, our purpose, what enlightenment is and is it attainable. At the time, I assumed I had heard it all in my quest for truth. I had been exposed to enough new age nonsense including Transcendental Meditation, all facets of conspiracy deception and its agenda and other rabbit holes that an overarching fear and confusion predominated in my psyche resulting in a sort of low-grade nihilism. None of what I learned brought me any conclusions or peace of mind that I had hoped might be attainable. This was the low point where my psoyca work began. The internal clearing techniques are astounding. Becoming a man of knowledge, the changes in my perceptions through knowings, the emotional balance or equanimity have all been truly transformative. I would say this work has brought me a higher sense of myself and freedom from herd mentality or hive virus programming I surely would never have known. Higher consciousness or enlightenment, I now realize, is clearing false programed beliefs and perceptions of the false ego, not some esoteric mystical gift.

I would describe doing this work as not just taking a simple Red Pill one and done transition from one belief to another. It is a course of many Red Pill doses over a period of time which consists of a careful and pragmatic examination of an individual's entire belief system resulting in higher cognitive and reasoning abilities, balancing of the emotional state and reevaluating one's relationship with first cog reality, thus then enabling one to advance to higher states of consciousness.

Based on my experience, I can attest that second cognition awareness is not handed to you, but with diligence and intent, you too can free yourself. I highly recommend this work to anyone with fortitude and a desire for real change.

Many thanks again to my teacher and friend Endall Beall for leading me out of the Matrix.

Arch Bramble

2019

Introduction

For over 2,500 years humanity has been deceived with a cognitive illusion where the concept of 'Enlightenment' is concerned. Siddhartha Gautama, more popularly known as the Buddha, is the first human being recognized to have attained this state of heightened cognitive awareness. Although he may not have been the first human being to discover this state of higher cognitive awareness, what I refer to as the Second Cognition, his experiences provide the first reported incident of this occurring written in human history.

Ever since the Indian Hindu philosophers, and particularly the Greek philosophers in the 7th century BC discovered a deceptive mind virus operating within the human body, the concept of 'spirit' emerged which has served as a major misdirection away from the Second Cognition state of awareness. In India, the Brahmans and Fakirs also made the discovery of this deceptive mind virus at the same time the Greek philosophers were discovering and interfacing with their inner *dæmons*, mistakenly believing that this *psyche*, was the 'Divine' human soul. Since those times and these grave mistakes in perceptual judgment, all of civilization followed down this road of misunderstanding about what they considered 'spirit, or the human 'soul'. I revealed this in exquisite detail in *The Truth About the 'Divine' Soul: The Late Creation of the Concept of Heaven*.

In the rush to false judgment about these inner *dæmons* and believing that they were the human soul, every world religion was spawned, and every religion worldwide has led mankind down a road to cognitive slavery and submission to an ideal that simply does not exist. We have devoted all our efforts in producing our books seeking to undo this false cognitive programming, providing no shortage of evidence with pragmatic and logical interpretations along the way, to try and help humanity free its consciousness from this false slavery of the mind. Sadly, there seems to be few who are genuinely interested, preferring to live with the false illusions of reality rather than mature and free their minds by facing the hard ugly truth.

In this book I will do my utter best to describe Second Cognition awareness, removing all the elements of supernaturalism, and explain to the reader in the most understandable terms possible what this higher state of perceptual awareness - Buddha's *Enlightenment* - actually is, and how it can work for everyone. Some of the concepts may sound sort of mystical, but that is only because the First Cognition state of awareness, which holds all humanity firmly grasped in its clutches, has no real touchstone of understanding to comprehend how this works. The primary focus of this book is to dispel the supernatural expectations and redirect the reader's understanding into the realm of perceptual comprehension in which it belongs, i.e. cognitive *pragmatism*.

There is no pragmatism where supernatural, mystical or occult beliefs are concerned. They have always been nothing but a lure, filled with expectations that have never paid off in the long run for humanity, or for those that seek spiritual enlightenment or salvation of their presumed souls. It is and has always been nothing more than a confidence racket, keeping priests, gurus and so-called occult adepts in positions of power over the ignorant masses who have chased the supernatural illusions for generations untold, no matter how many different ways these beliefs have been packaged over the ages.

Second Cognition awareness leads one to a higher state of perceptual awareness based strongly in pragmatism, observation, and critical thinking, which ultimately leads one to be able to extrapolate events from valid known data. This is not 'prophetic' abilities but is based in deductive reasoning. The concept of prophecy is just another faulty aspect of supernatural beliefs and expectations. It is the major thrust of this work to help those who have chosen this road to cognitive advancement understand what they are seeking without all the mystical hoopla and false expectations.

The terms Second Cognition, much like the word Enlightenment, brings with it, certain expectations, mostly based on thousands of years of supernatural or mystical desires foisted on humanity by the parasitic hapiym mind virus. From the standpoint of the mind virus infection, a *seer* was considered a mystic who had supernatural abilities and could speak to the spirits of the dead, angels, or even God. From the standpoint of the Second Cognition, a *seer* is an individual who has cleared all the cognitive detritus of the first Cognition world of illusion and freed their consciousness from the constraints of the first cognition world that serves as a harness on human perceptual awareness.

One must first understand the illusion before one can seek to transcend it within themselves. Although I have attacked this topic from many angles in my previous work, discussing the two definitions of ego and how one must slay the habits of the false ego created by the mind virus infection, I will seek to provide more in-depth explanations for understanding in this volume. My desire is that every reader can gain benefit from the journey in this book and come away with at least a better conceptual understanding of where this journey can lead you - *if* you have the stamina and courage enough to stay the course and see its benefits for you in the long run.

In my past presentations I have been compelled to recap information for cold readers. Starting with this book, this habit of recapping prior works in synopsized form comes to an end. For those who are unfamiliar with some of the principles and ideas presented in this book, you're just going to have to do the background work on your own. I am no longer going to engage in literary hand holding for those who have a narrow interest and think they can get the grasp of the grand tapestry of reality in one book or with one reading.

All of our books provide a broader perspective of reality than most of humanity is aware. One can't take in the scope of human history in one book. Libraries are filled worldwide with tomes of historical analysis. Within the realm of second cognition awareness the multiverse can unfold before them. To limited first cognition thinking and perceptions, what the second cognition can reveal to us will sound like science fiction or a horror story. Much in this book will sound like both. I am beyond seeking to make explanations for those whose worldview is predicated on compartmentalized propaganda, superficial impressions, uninformed opinions and horizontal linear perceptions of the world. The tapestry of the history of humanity on this planet is a sordid tale indeed, often sick making. Whether the reader choses to accept what is revealed in this book or not is not my concern. Every reader is asked to listen to their own inner guidance as to whether they accept these 'stories' or not. Just be prepared for what you will find in this book because much of it is going to be very unpleasant reading.

For those of our readers who have been diligent enough to read most or all of our books and are doing the hard work to advance their own consciousness, much of what you will find in these pages will provide more in-depth answers to questions you have probably had for some time. Some of this information will be more critical information to apply to your growth process, and a lot of it will be historical background covering many diverse areas of interest. For those who are doing the work and following our presentations, I want to offer thanks for your diligence.

1. What is the Second Cognition?

Having completed 36 books in our collected multiple series of books and companion volumes, one would think that we would have explained the second cognition more comprehensively than we have to date. The fact is that it has been explained every step of the way, yet I think false expectations lead people to believe second cognition awareness is something different than what it actually is. After thousands of years of mystical and supernatural thinking, humanity expects higher level awareness to be something of that nature. The false spiritual roads to alleged 'Enlightenment' are greatly at fault for these broadly accepted public spiritual misperceptions, and regardless of how we try to explain the second cognition otherwise, the desire and expectations for something mystical still overrides most people's perceptions on the matter.

Those who have read our full body of work have been taken on a journey into a realm of perceptual awareness that goes beyond the false illusionary world we think is reality. The concepts we present are highly challenging because they go against the constraints of layers of perceptual illusions that humanity *thinks* constitute reality. The fact is that we are all living in a carefully scripted movie, albeit enslaved against our will and fighting for our survival in this real-life drama we perceive is our reality.

I have written extensively about a cognitive mind virus and have provided what I think is substantial and irrefutable evidence of this virus' existence in human consciousness until very recently. Naturally, this goes against the grain of consensus reality, both in the religio-spiritual spectrum and equally in the realm of mainstream materialist scientism. Such a concept is too far outside our accepted notions of reality to be given credence by most of humanity at this stage of its cognitive evolution.

Equally as distasteful to the majority of Earth's population is the concept that human beings on this planet were genetically manufactured by offworld aliens and used our species as genetic lab rat experiments, which is the basis for all the racial variants we find on the planet. Although writers like Erich von Daniken and Zechariah Sitchin had much success convincing millions of people about their own theories of ancient alien intervention, the majority of Earth's population rejects such notions, despite ancient cuneiform tablets that relate such tales in abundance. It is easier to believe in a singular omniscient creator God who created the entire universe in a wondrous and miraculous 6 days, or that all life on this planet came from some single-celled creature that became life out of nothingness to provide the diversity of creatures on this planet, if you buy into Darwinian theory. If you look at the vast night sky, which of these three options makes the most logical sense? The latter two, which are the most accepted by religion and science, are both based on supernatural beliefs, no matter how hard science tries to convince us that life magically appeared from non-life to spawn every living creature on this planet from some enigmatic single-celled creature. Even if we consider the concept of panspermia, where some form of life seeded here from an asteroid strike carrying with it rudimentary life forms from which all the species on Earth grew and diversified in the Darwinian model, we have to ask where the lifeforms on such an asteroid originated? This is the conundrum of science and how it also resides on a foundation of faith more than truth, just like any other religion.

I intend to present a broad spectrum of information in this book that ideally should be weighed for consideration in seeking to expand the reader's perceptions. Every topic will not be discussed exhaustively, nor am I going to provide anything more than the information research necessary to share my observations and make my case. People already rely too much on so-called authoritative sources before they make up their minds, which is indicative of the obedience to authority syndrome present in all of humanity. This dependence on authority is programmed into our species after untold generations of humanity being a slave species, only knowing how to do what it's told to do by presumed authority figures, who very often in our current cultural milieu simply run on bluff and illusion garnering. You will never develop a free consciousness so long as you remain reliant on the opinions of other before you can make up your own mind on matters.

Throughout my work I have hammered home the idea that we live in a world of perceptual illusions. What this means is that, for the most part, we live in a world of *hearsay*. We shape our beliefs and even our inner identity on words written thousands of years ago that have ossified our consciousness. We shape our alleged education based on the hearsay of self-proclaimed 'teachers' who are themselves as mind-controlled as those they claim to educate. Humanity is not a species of genuinely free thinkers, particularly those academics who most loudly profess that they are. Everyone lives in cognitive boxes created and reinforced by our peer groups, family members, occupational associations, religious beliefs, political affiliations and accepted ideologies. The major rule of the fraudulent practice of psychology is to establish conformity for those who don't seem to fit comfortably into their cultural milieus and can be reshaped to 'cope' and once more become comfortable cogs as viable members of a cultural herd. Herd consciousness rules every mind on the planet. There is no genuine individuality because every individual measures themselves and their self-worth against the outside acceptance of their particular herd, and beliefs. The false inner ego is shaped by the need to please and conform to the external herd environment.

The road to the second cognition is designed to make real individuals out of herd animals. When every belief you harbor is dictated to you by others, every decision you make is predicated on whether it sits well within one's cultural mandates or not. Your determinations are predicated on what the herd will think if you do things that go against the accepted cultural consensus 'norms'. Herd ostracization keeps us all in line, walking in lockstep with the beliefs of our cultural peer groups. This is so bad that in some professional bailiwicks one can lose their livelihood if they don't toe the accepted narrative dictated by their profession. Academia, politics and psychology are at the top of this list of compelled professional performance. Religions do the same with those they consider heretics to their selective faiths. The threat of excommunication or expulsion from one's church or temple is usually enough to keep people in line to keep their mouths shut when contradicting the faith. In all the foregoing circumstances the herd rules the mind of the individual. Comply, or you will pay for it if you don't. The herd is nothing if not vindictive and hateful. Every herd knows how to enforce its will over every individual member. Fear of the herd reaction is what keeps everyone in check in every case. Fear is your primary enemy when seeking to become a cognitively free individual.

Ideally, this book will prove how little the 'real you' controls your thoughts, perceptions and decisions where your perceptual beliefs are concerned. Humans are all programmable machines. You can take a baby from any race anywhere in the world and place it in a foreign culture or society and it will grow up adopting the beliefs, language and traditions of that culture. This fact alone should illustrate how programmable human consciousness is, and also how adaptable it is. The sad thing is that we are programmed on multiple levels, the deepest levels of this programming being far out of our reach, unless we really dig for it and flush it out.

In our previous works we have supplied tools and explanations about how one can start challenging these illusionary perceptions and move toward freeing one's consciousness from the constraints of programmed perceptual reality. This book is going to focus more on the deeper housecleaning processes that get overlooked, as well as defining the problems that this deep housecleaning entails, provided one gets that far. The sad fact is that most people never get to that point of deep analysis and give up the process altogether well before they ever reach the stage of deeper analysis and uprooting the habits of the false ego. The success ratio in this process is tragically low. I won't lie to you with falsified odds for success in this endeavor. You are going to have to have guts and exquisite diligence to work with this continuing process to find success. You will also have to develop patience because nothing with this process happens as fast as our impatient ego desires wish for. Impatience and the desire for instantaneous results will also serve as a disappointing impediment to this process if you allow it to drive your expectations.

Expectations are also an enemy because nothing that we can imagine from a first cognition perspective will make you understand what second cognition awareness is. To start this process, everyone is shooting in the dark when creating the expectations on what this process will yield. These expectations are all based on historical cultural programming and we can only imagine things based on what the perceptual world presents to us as theoretical solutions. Your expectations will always come up short, so it is best to try and avoid expectations as much as possible during your growth process. Expectations always let you down because they rarely manifest.

No matter what your source material may be in the first cognition world, all consciousness studies bend toward the mystical, esoteric or supernatural because the first cognition world has no descriptive to explain the two differing states of cognitive awareness. Materialist science is convinced that consciousness resides specifically in the brain. It refuses to consider consciousness as anything more than a mechanical navigator of human life. Any concept of consciousness beyond the material human brain is anathema to this religion of materialist scientism.

All other consciousness studies find their basis in Platonic and Greek philosophical doctrines about their inner *dæmons,* what has erroneously been defined as the human soul for the last 2,700 years or so. Religious concepts of the soul all find their origin with early Greek and Hindu thinking, which I feel I effectively proved in *The Truth About the 'Divine' Soul: The Late Creation of the Concept of Heaven.* These beliefs, initiated by Plato in the West, are also deeply rooted in every modern spiritual and religious belief system on the planet. The Theosophical Society with its alleged Ascended Masters is only a continuation of the Platonic dialogue with one's inner *dæmon,* which was nothing more than a parasitic invasive mind virus, as I have tirelessly explained in many of my works to date.

It is from Plato's philosophy of the cosmic 'divine' Monad that the concept of a singular God or idea of cosmic Oneness originates. Although the heretic Pharaoh Akhenaten, may have proposed the first concept of monotheism with his state worship of the sun got Aten, it wasn't until the 7th century BC that the concept of Heaven was created, which has permeated every religious and spiritual tradition on the planet ever since. It was only through Plato's writings and the composition of the Hindu *Upanishads* at roughly the same time in the East that the concept about the alleged divine human 'soul' planted its deepest roots. There is no such thing as a human divine soul as people perceive one to exist. It is a fabrication, a poison contrived by the hapiym mind virus to keep humanity ever searching outside itself for magical supernatural solutions and keeps humanity totally willing to give up its humanness to the mystical lie of an eternal future for the human personality. With roughly 2/3 or more of the people on this planet embracing such beliefs, this is one of the major cognitive lies that must eventually be overcome, but that most are simply too fearful to let go of. It is also one of the major stumbling blocks that creates what I call a *red line* that people are utterly unwilling to cross to attain their cognitive freedom.

Because all of humanity was infected with this parasitic cosmic mind virus, we all suffer from the symptomatology of its infectious nature. As much as every human personality is shaped by its experiences and cultural programming, we have all been infected with the residuals of this cosmic parasitic virus which was a collective 'mind'. Carl Jung defined this as the collective unconscious. Although he never perceived this mind virus in his theory for the collective unconscious, it is in fact the common feature that has subliminally programmed humanity since its creation. For one to free their consciousness from the residual infectious symptoms of this virus infection, to eliminate and kill the residual cognitive habits installed by this invasive mind virus is a prerequisite.

The invasive hapiym mind virus, which infected us right after birth, adapted itself to its new environment, our physical form, and started duplicating our personality as we grew and matured. The virus fed on our emotions, so it learned how to manipulate our nervous system to generate emotional responses to keep itself fed. Aside from the cultural programming through external sources, we all carry this virus form of internal emotional programming, and a false doppelganger personality began to grow and convinced us that this false virus personality is actually who we are. This false virus personality keeps us in line with its fabricated beliefs about itself by triggering our emotions to protect this false inner image – the ego. The negative emotions are the most powerful tools the virus used against us to keep itself supreme in our minds – fear, guilt, shame, insecurity, doubt, etc. It is through finding and eliminating all the programs that trigger these kinds of emotions within us that leads one to a higher state of free consciousness.

Your emotions have been the control mechanism through which the hapiym mind virus controlled your mind and kept its false personality in place to rule your consciousness. The virus lived and fed itself on superficial belief systems. Any time anyone chose to buck these beliefs, once they became stiffly embedded in our minds through cultural programming, fear was usually the emotion used by the virus against you to make sure you didn't reject the adopted belief system. The whole purpose of the mind virus was to not only feed on you, but to also feed whatever collective herd you belonged to – all for the *greater good*. The herd was more important than the self. We have all been exquisitely programmed to think of the herd first and ourselves second. As such, we are not independent individuals, but herd animals used to fulfill the hive virus' designs and have been throughout all human history.

To become a truly cognitively free entity, a *true* individual, requires getting rid of all this programming, both internally created by the hive virus and externally by our cultures. You will never be cognitively free so long as who you think you are is shaped by herd consensus through tradition, race, national identity, religious identity or political identity. Each of these aspects of your internal false personality are merely shadows of who you can become. Everyone is a programmed biological robot, and no one is willing to admit this gruesome fact. This is why psychological programming and warfare are so effective in controlling the masses. Regardless of how much you proclaim to be an individual, you are as malleable as soft clay in the hands of skilled psychological manipulators. Just saying these things may cause an inner emotional reaction and a sense of denial to face these harsh truths. If you are experiencing this, then it is the residual virus emotional habits that create these emotional misgivings as well as your denial. To believe these things challenges the inner false ego image created by the virus itself. These reactions are as predictable as the sunrise --- *in everyone!*

Although the original Greek word *psyche* translates to mean 'soul', in modern public understanding it is generally perceived to represent the overall mind or inner being, which serves as the basis for the industry of modern psychology. When I use the word psyche within the pages of this book, I am not referring to the hive cell *dæmon* or soul, but the overall composite nature of the human mind.

The fact that this invasive parasitic mind virus could influence and impact every human being's consciousness should readily illustrate that your mind is not totally your own. If this mind virus could create a replica false ego of your personality and make you believe that this false ego is you, are you really who you think you are, or are you simply following the internal dictates of a parasitic mind virus impersonating you and controlling not only your emotions but your very perceptions of yourself? The answer to this should be patently obvious, uncomfortable as accepting this premise may be. What will further be illustrated is how the field of psychology is an utter sham and that no one practicing with a psychology or psychiatric degree knows jack shit about how to heal the human psyche, despite all the commercialization to convince the public that they do. Every one of these so-called professionals is just as infected with the residuals of the mind virus as you are and equally as locked into the first cognition realm of illusions.

Contrary to all the mystical traditions that have been preached about advancing consciousness and achieving Oneness with the cosmos, the second cognition leads one to total sobriety where cognitive perception is concerned. There is nothing magical or mystical about it. It is only perceived that way from first cognition limited perceptions in a world based purely on perceptual images and projecting our own false ego image onto the face of the world to gain cultural acceptance within our selective herds. Because the first cognition system of awareness has nothing to compare itself to in understanding second cognition awareness, second cognition awareness can't be fully comprehended no matter how it is explained or who has sought to explain it. It is only the continued *experiences* brought about through the internal clearing process that moves one closer to that state of cognitive freedom and emotional equanimity that comes with second cognition advanced consciousness. I am going to do my best in this volume to provide more comprehensive information about this process for those whose intent is to ultimately succeed and break the reins of the first cognition harness on their consciousness.

The second cognition state of awareness requires individuals, not herds. Humans, like many other animals, are social beings, but it was the virus that *socialized* us into herd clusters. One can be an independent individual consciousness and be quite social without being socialized into mandated herd compliance. This is a major part of what second cognition awareness will bring you.

2. Explaining Self-importance

The issue of self-importance revolves specifically around the hapiym virus infection. Every human is self-interested, and there is nothing wrong with pursuing one's self-interests. As self-contained autonomous beings living within our own skin, survival is a self-interest prerogative programmed into the human form on the deepest level, as it is with any living creature. What the hapiym mind virus did was to capitalize on this base human programing, fear – or the fight or flight mechanism, and twist it to its own survival. It turned survival self-interest into false ego self-importance. The self-importance every human exhibits is a result of the mind virus turning our survival instinct into *its* survival instinct by making itself, (the false secondary illusionary ego), more important than it could ever be on its own.

To understand the mind virus ego replica, just imagine it as being a duplicate of your personality on steroids. Everything that makes you a good person in your mind is amplified and distorted out of proportion, and everything bad about yourself that you want buried and kept from public knowledge is equally amplified out of proportion. Through this artificially amplified emotional doppelganger, every human being has been forced to relinquish much of their primary personality and subject themselves to the mind virus replica that resides within us.

Through amplifying the emotion of fear, specifically, the mind virus was able to control our minds. When you can understand this principle about an amplified false personality – a genuine alter ego – then you can conceptualize how all of humanity operates in a state of constant self-delusion, not only presenting a false image to the world, but also by lying to ourselves to satisfy the virus' false persona within. Where fight or flight is a matter of the survival of the form, the fight or flight mechanism has been twisted to protect the false persona of the hapiym hive cell that lived within us.

There are two primary objectives when one is working to achieve the second cognition state of cognitive advancement, and that is removing the perceptual illusions that we believe are the world in which we live; and the second aspect of this process is destroying the inner illusions we have all adopted about ourselves believing we are the false mind virus personality. As a defense strategy, the virus programmed every human mind to protect *its* false personality by altering our emotional habits as a protective mechanism that don Juan referred to as self-importance.

Self-importance is a symptom of the virus' false personality itself, and it is distinct from the self-interest of the fight or flight programming for survival of our bodies. This infection called self-importance is also what we call self-image. To the virus-infected human waking state ego, your natural personality, the hapiym virus is a bloated false ego that thrives on fear of discovery and uses our natural human traits and bends them to its will to protect it from being discovered for the sham personality it is.

In the world of the hive virus' collective intelligence, we all thrive on illusions about other people – the *image* of how they present themselves to the public. Every human being presents this false image to every other human being. We all shape our perceptions most of the time on superficial judgments based on this image reliance. 'The clothes make the man' is one of the most exemplary notions about self-image. We often judge by appearance quicker than by allowing ourselves to listen to anyone and learning anything about them first. As such, we all operate in a world driven by illusion and superficial appearance. Yet, when we analyze this appearance, we very often discover that we are wrong in our perceptions. We all feed the same superficial illusions to one another – 'I wouldn't be caught dead in that outfit!' is another prime example of living in a world of superficial illusions based purely on image projection.

People select their clothing much of the time to project these images, wearing campaign hats or buttons, T-shirts with sayings that we feel reflect what we think and things of that nature. All of these actions, like dressing up on Sunday to go to church, are about feeding an illusion to the hapiym-infected herds we choose to associate with and feed them an image that they expect to see as a symbol of solidarity with these selective herds. The world feeds us illusions and we feed illusions back onto the world that we want the world to perceive about us and make the appropriate judgment in accordance with our self-image and self-importance. The same can be said about status symbols of all kinds - cars, houses, awards, titles, degrees, you name it. Every one of these items is designed to project an image that we want to transmit to the public in our quest for self-importance, driven solely by the mind virus' yearning for acceptance by the herd.

By explaining all this, then perhaps you can better understand what don Juan meant when he said, "Self-importance is our greatest enemy. Think about it--what weakens us is feeling offended by the deeds and misdeeds of our fellow men. Our self-importance requires that we spend most of our lives offended by someone. Every effort should be made to eradicate self-importance from the lives of warriors. Without self-importance we are invulnerable."

Self-importance spawns from the false ego of the hapiym mind virus. Every insecurity we have about ourselves 'is a direct product of the mind virus infection. We can't be ourselves because we are too preoccupied with protecting the insecure self-image of the hapiym virus false persona. When we get offended and get defensive, we are not defending ourselves, we are defending the insecure false persona of the virus. The more we work to undermine these false impressions and beliefs about ourselves that are the symptoms of the virus, the freer our minds become and the more our consciousness starts to shift into a higher state of awareness.

Every mystical tradition on this planet was spawned by the mind virus collective itself. The false personality of the virus convinced humanity that it was our 'soul', performing one of the greatest feats of deception imaginable in the annals of humanity's existence. Don Juan referred to the tactics of this mind virus predator from the stars as a 'stupendous feat' because 'it gave us its mind'. Truer words were never spoken as a warning for humanity about this parasitic predator. Not only did the virus give humanity its collective 'mind', but it gave us every bad emotional habit ever exhibited by any human being that ever lived.

As I explained in prior works, the hapiym virus had no personality of its own, it had no mind of its own except what it could steal and replicate from the human personality it infected. Thus, the virus collective was only a singular collective of every human personality that ever lived. The virus was just a recording device that could only emulate the personality of its host after the human host died, forever caught in a state of arrested development after the death of its human host. Any given hive cell was a duplicate of a human life lived, and when the human host died, the hive cell ceased to develop. It was like a bubble containment field of the personality it infected, forever trapped in the final moments when the host died. There was no growth, there was no advancement for a hive cell after the death of its host. It was nothing more than the storybook of an individual's lifetime and that is all it would ever be. When the host died the story ended. All it could do is carry the memories of its host and live them over and over again for eternity because the virus had no mind of its own.

I have drifted astray somewhat and need to get back on track explaining how one overcomes the virus habits, which are mostly emotional. The hapiym virus fed off our emotions, so the habits of the virus embedded in our physiology are all emotionally volatile when we seek to remove them. Because the necessity to defend the false ego personality of the virus is deeply embedded in our body and mind, confronting these habits within ourselves is always fraught with psychological and emotional disruption. We don't want to admit things about ourselves that the virus made us believe. It capitalized on self-doubt and fed us large doses of defeatism to ensure that we never found the strength to confront its dominion over our minds. Denial is one of its strongest weapons to keep our consciousness subdued to its will. Denial of our bad habits is usually the first avenue of retreat that keeps most of us in check. By bad habits I am not talking about physical habits, I am talking about emotional and mental habits.

If we can start to move past the denial protective mechanism of the false personality, then guilt and shame are standing in the shadows as more powerful weapons of fear to keep us from facing the virus symptoms that lie buried within us head on. The virus, after eons of inhabiting humanoid forms, knew exactly how to manipulate its hosts to perform its will against us and to its sole advantage. The first stages of unraveling the habits and illusions of the world of the virus usually start by challenging our perceptions about the outside world.

People have been intentionally steered away from believing any kind of conspiracy theory, for instance, particularly in the present era based on a lot of psychological programming by the CIA to defame anyone who entertains such ideas. When one is generally faced with conspiracy theories, and they start to believe any of them, whether real or contrived propaganda, it has the tendency to drive a wedge into the world of perceptual illusion. It cracks the mirror. For those with wisdom who can find genuine, verifiable conspiracy fact, the way their world of illusion starts to fall apart is when the individual asks themselves, 'If I was wrong about this, what else am I wrong about?" It is this sense of inquiry that will lead the seeker deeper into the rabbit hole of self-discovery. Without such inquisitiveness, one is not going to proceed very far on the road to the second cognition.

In saying this, I must put a qualifier on this. Because the world of illusion is founded on *beliefs*, one can adopt a conspiracy theory, or set of ideas, that is wholly erroneous. Even though the concept may be contrived propaganda, it can still be useful if one doesn't just accept the conspiracy notion and park their mentality in just another belief system, which is most often the case. It is a continued sense of inquiry that is going to move you forward, for resting in one belief system only leaves one stuck there, exchanging one set of beliefs for another. Regardless of the belief, if it *is* a belief, it is still built on a foundation of sand, which can eventually be eroded with deeper inquiry. Lacking a sense of inquiry, parking our minds in any given belief system, will still leave us firmly rooted in the first cognition world of illusion.

As I have stated numerous times in previous works, one must constantly ask, '*Why* do I believe what I believe?' In time this should ultimately lead to asking yourself why you believe what you believe about yourself, not just the outside world. This will lead to the process of internal self-analysis and flushing out the virus habits of the false self-image as well as the false sense of virus induced self-importance. This is not a sequential process where one must erode the perceptual beliefs of the outside world then turn inward, they can both be done simultaneously in stages.

We live in a world that we believe provides us choices. In most cases these choices are dictated to us by others. They are more like menu options that someone places before us from which we must choose. Much of the time they are not genuine choices, but illusionary perception options to accept one belief over another. One might consider this type of perceptual reality-shopping as living in a mall, with a multitude of shops and products (beliefs) to choose from, thinking this mall is the greater reality. Using this model, we all become programmed to accept these limited perceptions of reality, even defending these illusions. The primary objective to attaining the second cognition state of awareness is to not stay lost in this mall of menus, but to get out of the mall altogether and make our own choices.

Within this cognitive mall, there are expected modes of behavior, and it is these modes of behavior that establish our habits, both emotionally and mentally. Everyone within the mall uses the same rules of conditioned behavior regardless of which shop they are in or what brand of belief the shop is selling to its herd customers. This is the herd mentality. There is a specific range of conditioned responses that all humans choose from in their emotional behavior. Each individual may have different triggers that incite joy, anger, fear or depression, but the range of conditioned emotional behavior is the same in every human being, barring the psychopath who has no physiological mechanism that ties into emotions.

For every one of us, our sense of self-importance springs from this mall-like environment of emotional sameness. It also shapes our internal self-image based on a combination of peer pressure, herd programming for conformity, acceptance of consensus perceptions of reality, and how our experiences shape our emotions in the face of these external programming pressures. The external world delivers the programming on many levels, and our experiences are interpreted through this programming. Negative experiences that go against the herd cultural indoctrination can shock the consciousness, which implants and embeds programs in the cellular memory, which is the body's memory database. No matter what you may remember or forget in your brain, the cell system and the body remember it *all*.

These embedded programs, based on negative experience, set the stage for our emotional development and reactions throughout our lives. Most of the time when we get emotionally triggered we have no clue as to the basis for what makes us explode in anger, fear or defensiveness. The triggers are buried in the cellular memory and the brain has no clue what sparks these emotional outbursts when they occur. The con game called psychology has not figured this out. Psychologists have figured out how to program the mind through propaganda, peer pressure and compelled cultural performance. As such, psychology has been used as a weapon to program humanity and its emotions over the last century of developing the field of psychology.

When we combine what the mind virus did to all of us through its internal manipulation, and you couple it with the need to fit into our cultural herd environments at all levels, then you understand how humanity's mind and emotions have been socially engineered to be nothing more than self-indulgent and self-important illusionary creatures functioning only on the level of presenting a false self-image for the consumption of others within the herd network.

Having stated the foregoing, we find the first area of instinctual self-delusion that initiates when our beliefs are challenged, is with utter denial of these facts, and facts they are. We are so convinced that we are this cartoon character we call 'me', that we will defend it, with violence if necessary. Until one is even willing to consider this ugly truth about the hive false ego, they will go nowhere on the path to alleged enlightenment. To succeed in this process, one must be *brutally* honest with themselves. As don Juan honestly stated, "Self-importance can't be fought with niceties." If you aren't willing to be rough on yourself there is no point in engaging the process at all. Friedrich Nietzsche stated as much in his writings. This isn't work for lightweights. It requires being ruthless with oneself while dredging up all the falsehoods and programs that lay harbored deep within our cellular programming.

We all embrace a self-image about ourselves – about how nice we are, or how compassionate we are, or how devout we are to our particular faiths or political ideologies. The level of belief we place in these external perceptions works in tangent with supporting our self-image. We do not just believe the belief, we *become* the belief, or at best, a defender of the belief, because to challenge the belief challenges who we think we are as individuals. The external and internal belief systems become intertwined and inseparable. The more fiercely we defend the beliefs and dig our heels in protecting them, the deeper the self-programming embeds on the cellular level, and the greater the sense of self-importance ratchets up to protect the beliefs which also becomes a rigid part of our false self-image. Through this process we all become our own worst enemies, yet this enemy is the one we must each confront and defeat to attain second cognition awareness.

For those who have read our other material and are familiar with cell talk and the cellular instructions we provided in *Demystifying the Mystical* and *The Second Cognition Toolbox*, the best time to address uninstalling cellular programs that trigger negative emotions is when you encounter the emotions. While your emotions are engaged, issuing cellular instructions to uninstall any and all programs that are connected to whatever negative emotions may arise is the best time to remove such programs and their triggers. While your emotions are engaged, your cellular memory can go right to the source program causing the emotional discomfort and uninstall the program. One must, however, be firm in their mental conviction that they want the programmed removed as well. If the mind is unwilling to give up the program, particularly if it is associated with the false self-image, it will create a conflict between the mind and the cellular memory and the cellular instructions and may well result in no progress.

One doesn't always need to know the exact source for what triggers these emotional reactions, only that they want the programs gone. One can agonize over trying to find the source for every program that generates these emotional responses, but if your emotions are already engaged, it is best to not bother trying to discover the source of the discomfort, because very often the program is embedded so deeply you will never find its source. Our incessant curiosity and need to know everything can often work against us if we try to overanalyze the situation and miss the opportunity to remove a 'live' program when our emotions are engaged.

Another thing you must be aware of in this process is that the deeper you go in destroying the virus false self-image and its emotional habits is that the emotions become more subtle. Unlike programs that generate large emotional outbursts, many of these deeper emotional responses are of a more subtle nature and can often only be sensed as a squirming feeling of internal discomfort. The need to get defensive over protecting the idea of the self-image is also a good emotional indicator of these subtler programs. This includes more subtle inner feelings of shame, guilt or denial over facing some of our deeper emotional habits. It takes some practice to start sensing these deeper and subtler emotions, but with a few incidents of encountering them the hallmarks are relatively easy to detect. The hard part is finding the willingness to face these discomforts and resolve the inner emotional issues. Since they will be associated with intimately held beliefs about oneself and their self-image, you should expect inner conflict from the programming. When we deny that we are doing what these programs reveal to us, the denial itself only leaves the self-important self-image of the false ego firmly in place. You are not this image, but if you don't overcome your own denial, you will never get these issues resolved.

A trickier part of this process is learning how the virus habits have taught us skillful excuse-making, or rationalizations that the false ego employs to defend itself. We fall into a mental process of rationalizing how the false self-image is really us and why we shouldn't remove the programs of self-importance. In such cases of circular logic rationalizing, focusing more acutely on the why you believe what you believe about yourself can lead you to a resolution, provided your rationalizing process doesn't talk you out of it altogether. This is the more slippery aspect of the false hive persona and it is also the hardest part to overcome. We all use a form of self-justification to keep the false ego and its habits firmly in place. If you find yourself in this mental loop of self-justification, it is only the false bravado of the hive self-image justifying its self-importance in your mind. Self-justification is still defending the false ego and it still amounts to excuse making. The bad thing is that this habit of self-justification is deeply embedded in our psyche and we do it almost as a first-nature habit. We do it so consistently with ourselves, defending and justifying our own actions in our mind, that we don't even know that it is a residual defense mechanism of the virus persona itself. Until you can become aware of this self-justified defending of your inner beliefs, it will run you in circles and the virus habits will still control your mind and your emotions related to whatever it is you are defending and justifying to yourself. Through this self-justification process, you can talk yourself into or out of anything your self-important ego self-image demands to keep in place. Any part of you that needs to defend itself is part of the false ego self-image.

As I have stated in prior works, you are seeking a state of emotional equanimity, meaning being rid of all the virus' habits of emotional volatility and reaching a state of having nothing to defend. If you are defending any belief and have to justify it to yourself, you are defending the false ego self-image and the illusions it embraces as its perceptual reality. As a fully functional human being you should not have to defend who you are. The only thing that ever needed defending or was open to be offended was the virus personality itself. Every ounce of energy you contribute to feeding these emotions is an energy draw on your form and your consciousness. One will not have freedom of thought so long as we allow reactive emotions and inner defense mechanisms to steal our very real peace of mind. The fact is that humanity spends so much of its time defending this false ego image and being offended when its ideas are affronted, that peace of mind and emotional equanimity are an unimaginable illusion to virtually everyone. Yet, this is the state of awareness that leads to second cognition higher-level perceptions. So long as you are literally chained down by the energy used to support all these emotions, you will not have the cognitive freedom you seek. You will be a slave to your emotions and the ideas and beliefs that trigger those emotions.

One final aspect I want to cover in this chapter is what is referred to as silence of the mind or stilling the inner dialogue. The incessant chatter that goes on in our heads is a result of the false persona filling our heads with doubt, fears and worries. All of these incessant thoughts that keep our minds in turmoil are a result of part of us arguing with the false persona and all its fears. As one removes more and more of the programs that create the inner emotional conflicts, there will be less conflict in our minds. When we remove the emotional programs that cause these anxieties and worries that keep us continually talking to ourselves in our minds, this inner dialogue will eventually shut down on its own and you will find that silence of the mind you seek.

Gaining silence of the mind does not mean that your brain is going to go defunct or that you will stop thinking, because we all need to think as a necessary function to navigate the world. What is means is that all the incessant worry and anxiety that poses these never-ending questions in our minds will come to an end and one will gain clarity of thought, where their thinking processes can be used appropriately rather than being abused by the virus habits we all employ to protect that false self-image. In like kind, by removing the programs that trigger our emotions does not mean that you will be emotionless. Instead you will be in charge of your emotions and will employ them when you choose, not when the virus habits arbitrarily dictate programmed emotional reactions. When I say that you are in control of your emotions, I do not mean that you have to actively work to control them. Once the virus habits are removed, then your emotions return to what would be their natural state without the virus infection.

Our emotions are a navigation tool, just like the other five senses. It is a sixth sense, as I think I effectively proved in *Emotionalism: How the Human Herds are Controlled*. Instead of being led around by the neck through volatile emotions, emotional balance takes place on its own when one loses all need to defend the false image or be offended by the actions or words of others. So long as we are controlled by the programs that trigger these emotional outbursts, whether internally or externally, the virus habits control your emotional landscape. Once one rids themselves of these programs, just as with the inner dialogue, your emotions will reset to their natural state of equanimity on their own. The more of these pernicious programs you remove, you should start to notice a gradual difference in your emotional demeanor. It will provide cumulative examples to you as you lose more and more of the emotional volatility programmed into you as your emotional trigger point programs are removed and uninstalled.

With all the information provided in this chapter, then the reader should understand the basis for self-importance, the false self-image of the virus secondary ego, and gain understanding on some of the subtler deprogramming processes to use to finally arrive at becoming a person with nothing to defend. The more energy you reclaim by not feeding these pernicious reactive emotional programs, the more clarity of mind and peace of mind you will achieve paving the road to higher cognitive advancement. As I stated, this is a *process*, not a goal. It takes time, and no matter how you try you can't hurry the process. Also, the process is ongoing until one gives up on themselves. The problem with most people is that they don't have the patience to stick with the process.

3. Becoming a Person of Knowledge

I am not going to expend a lot of energy on this chapter because I covered most of the explanations in *Beyond Don Juan: Into the Third Attention – The Second Cognition*. I am, however, going to go over some of these points again because they can stand to be reiterated and they are very important for one advancing their awareness.

Most people live in compartmentalized boxes of perception. Their world is ordered and usually very finite. Where I utilized the teaching of don Juan in the *Beyond Don Juan* book, I am going to share some observations along similar lines from Friedrich Nietzsche below. These excerpted passages come from *The Gay Science, section 347*:

> ***"Believers and their need to believe.****- How much one needs a **faith** in order to flourish, how much that is "firm" and that one does not wish to be shaken because one **clings** to it, that is a measure of the degree of one's strength (or. to put the point more clearly, of one's weakness)."*

> *"Metaphysics is still needed by some; but so is that impetuous **demand for certainty** that*

*today discharges itself among large numbers of people in a scientific-positivistic form. The demand that one wants by all means that something should be firm (while on account of the ardor of this demand one is easier and more negligent about the demonstration of this certainty)-this, too, is still <u>the demand for a support, a prop</u>, in short, that **instinct of weakness** which, to be sure. does not create religious, metaphysical systems, and convictions of all kinds but--conserves them."*

*"Faith always coveted most and needed most urgently where will is lacking; for will. as the affect of command, is the decisive sign of sovereignty and strength. In other words, the less one knows how to command, the more urgently one covets someone who commands. who commands severely - a god, prince, class, physician, father confessor, dogma, or party conscience. From this one might perhaps gather that the two world religions. Buddhism and Christianity. may have owed their origin and above all their sudden spread to a tremendous collapse and **disease of the will**. And that is what actually happened: both religions encountered a situation in which the will had become diseased. giving rise to a demand that had become utterly desperate for some "thou shalt." Both religions taught fanaticism in ages in*

which the will had become exhausted, and thus they offered innumerable people some support. a new possibility of willing, some delight in willing. For fanaticism is the only will, "strength of the will" that even the weak and insecure can be brought to attain, being a sort of hypnotism of the whole system of the senses and the intellect for the benefit of an excessive nourishment (hypertrophy) of a single point of view and feeling that henceforth becomes dominant-which the Christian calls his **faith**. *Once a human being reaches the fundamental conviction that he* **must** *be commanded. he becomes "a believer." Conversely, one could conceive of such a pleasure and power of self-determination, such a* **freedom** *of the will that the spirit would take leave of all faith and every wish for certainty, being practiced in maintaining himself on insubstantial ropes and possibilities and dancing even near abysses. Such a spirit would be the* **free spirit** *par excellence."*

[Emphasis in original]

What Nietzsche observes in these passages is the hapiym virus' effect on the human psyche and how most of humanity lives. We are all subservient to the 'obedience to authority' programming that plagues every world society where people have abrogated being educated to their higher-ups who they expect to do the thinking for them, then hand down dictates of behavior, morals and cultural ideologies from on high. Through these observations, Nietzsche has pointed out that humanity has relinquished its right to think for itself. It has abrogated its responsibility to be an informed individual and passed that responsibility on to others. Let the leaders dictate the faith and I will follow, regardless of whether it is religious, political, one of traditions or cultural mandates. Someone, *anyone*, do the thinking for me then tell me what to do and I will follow your lead! This is humanity on the global scale. This is the herd cluster mindset of the hapiym collective mind.

Because humanity has given up the will to make its own decisions for itself, intellectual abusers and the elite have taken that responsibility and further insulated their presumed superiority, as priests, academics, politicians or bureaucrats by instructing the masses how they should behave according to their mandates of varying 'faiths'. Faith is not to be construed in strictly the religious sense. Any time anyone believes in an ideological illusion and defends the ideology, then they are operating wholly on faith, just as these passages by Nietzsche point out. One can either live in a world of faith and illusions, believing something is true because some chosen authority or writings tells us it is so, or we can become persons of knowledge and relinquish the obedience to authority syndrome that rules our consciousness and become our own authorities over our own minds and lives.

One will never become a person of knowledge simply being a believer maintaining a limited faith. You will only be a sheep living in a corral created for your consciousness dictated by others. The claims made by people about who they 'follow' exemplifies this state of cognitive submission. You will never lead yourself so long as you follow the authority of someone else willing to dictate to you what you should do, believe, and how to think in herd comformity. In such situations, the individual is as easy to steer through their emotions than through any genuine thought processes. Every faith demands emotional devotion and ultimately defending. Recognizing this need to defend all articles of faith shows you that these faiths are the illusionary realms of the hapiym collective mind virus. Truth doesn't need defending because it is what it is. Only faiths and beliefs need defending by their followers who have adopted their particular faiths as part of their false ego personalities.

Don Juan taught that believing is a cinch – having to believe takes effort. Having to believe amounts to weighing all the available information then making a decision on what to believe in the face of that information. That is *having* to believe. One will never be able to make an informed decision embracing only the information of their faith. Most people do not even know the opposing side, they just know they don't like whatever it is, and most dislike their opposition because it threatens their faith and limited worldview. Emotions play a key role in the decision-making processes of the faithful, more so than pragmatic investigation and *having* to believe.

Because of thousands of generations of mystical beliefs shoved down our throat by the hapiym mind virus, people can scarcely perceive the value of higher-level second cognition awareness and how it can be used to better navigate our lives as human beings. People are more interested in woo-woo concepts about advanced consciousness and mucking about 'out there' in the cosmos than they seem to be interested in pragmatically using advanced cognitive awareness in how to better navigate through life on this planet using second cognition consciousness. The mystical fantasy greatly outweighs any thoughts about pragmatic application of advanced cognitive awareness.

It's easy for any of us to sit back and agree with these observations, so long as we are looking at others when we nod our agreement. It is an entirely different animal when we have to admit that we do the selfsame things ourselves. First cognition consciousness is almost cookie-cutter patterns across the spectrum. This is one reason sinister elite psychologists know how to program and socially engineer human consciousness. You are equally as programmed and programmable as 'they' are. We can readily point to 'them' and say, 'yes, I can see that in the herd', but we refuse to acknowledge that we are just as guilty of the same cognitive habits and subject to the same emotional programming as all those around us. It is this refusal to look into our own inner mirror and admit these things that keeps us walking in lockstep with the rest of our cultural herds. This is not being a person of knowledge; this is being a programmed robot.

To become a person of knowledge one must willfully seek to expand their knowledge base. Look into things you know nothing about. The most progress you will make will be found in forcing yourself to study opposing opinions and ideologies, not reading things that confirm your foregone conclusions about your particular ideological faiths. Your worldview will never expand so long as you insist on fitting everything you see and read into your foregone conclusion boxes. The object of cognitive advancement is to expand your awareness, not compress whatever you are confronted with into your limited perceptual boxes. If you can develop and hone working with your psoyca sentience, your opportunities for cognitive expansion unfold exponentially the more you expand your knowledge base.

Moving into new and often distasteful areas of research will provide you opportunities for insights you can scarcely imagine from your present level of cognitive awareness. The subsequent chapters in this book are going to take you down into some dark recesses of human history that the average person doesn't generally want to consider. You are going to have to have a strong stomach to face some of these facts. Contrary to all the spiritual fluff and rainbows, reality is substantially grittier and uglier than humanity wants to admit operating within the safe borders of their selected beliefs on faith and sanitized history. What I will be sharing in the rest of this book are stories that will explain why humanity has regressed willfully into ignorance and why elite academics, historians and politicians work tirelessly to make us accept their sanitized historical narratives. The historical narratives are 'safer' than the ugly truth that many of these elite controllers are fully aware of. Fasten your seatbelts, you are about to embark on a journey into second cognition pragmatism and face the sordid reality of human history.

4. Some Ugly History

I am going to open this chapter with another set of observations by Friedrich Nietzsche from *Beyond Good and Evil*:

> *"How we have made everything around us clear and free and easy and simple! how we have been able to give our senses a passport to everything superficial, our thoughts a god like desire for wanton pranks and wrong inferences!— how from the beginning, we have contrived to retain our ignorance in order to enjoy an almost inconceivable freedom, thoughtlessness, imprudence, heartiness, and gaiety—in order to enjoy life! And only on this solidified, granitelike foundation of ignorance could knowledge rear itself hitherto, the will to knowledge on the foundation of a far more powerful will, the will to ignorance, to the uncertain, to the untrue!"*

For 1,700 years the western world has shaped its reality based on an utter set of lies. This set of lies is established with the false history of the Hebrews presented in the Bible. Every aspect of western thought, whether for or against Christianity, is predicated upon this fraudulent history that never happened with the exception of a few verifiable episodes folded into the fictional narrative. This is the primary foundation of ignorance upon which all of western knowledge is built. I hate to tell you folks, but you've been had. Your world perception is built on a contrived set of lies which all sides of the equation support out of fear of retribution for challenging and destroying the myth. There are those Atheists who challenge the narrative, mostly from the standpoint of disparaging the story about the neurotic imaginary God, but few really put a full-hearted effort into exposing the historical lies. There is too much political power to challenge by exposing the mythology and billions of believers that would hang you from the gallows if you tell them their entire system of faith is based on lies fabricated to control their consciousness and make them slaves to an illusion.

There are numerous scholars who have accurately noted that many of the stories folded into the Bible come from more ancient Sumerian origins that predated the alleged history of the Hebrews by thousands of years, but they still do not directly challenge the false history of the Jews as an utter lie. The more the archaeologists dig in Israel, the less they find that supports the mythical biblical narrative. Naturally you can't get people of faith to accept these facts, especially when they have formed their own biased type of investigation called Biblical Archaeology. Archaeology is archaeology. By claiming it is biblical only shows the tribal bias to confirm the belief system. There can be no objective conclusions reached when every tiny scrap of evidence that might, just maybe, possibly confirm the narrative basis of their faith. To expect unbiased reporting about such things is rather ludicrous if you think about it.

From our modern perspective we can't put ourselves into the heads of our ancestors. When you think about the early Christians, for instance, we cast our perceptions back into their minds and think we know how and what they thought and believed. For an assessment on the fraud of Christianity you might want to look into a book called *Bamboozled! Besieged by Lies, Man Never a Sinner: How World Leaders Use Religion to Control the Populace* by Timothy Aldred. I wouldn't put it on a required reading list, but it is a pretty serious critical analysis of the faults found in Pauline Christianity for those interested.

In the ancient world, virtually every country was vying for the antiquity of their country, city state or their race. Each of these places claimed their premier gods and the origin of their specific peoples traced back to the cultural formulators as sons of specific gods or as offspring of demigods. Rome traced its antiquity to the famed Romulus and Remus, the twins purported suckled by a she-wolf. The varying Greek tribes did the same thing as did other areas around the world. The bragging rights of these peoples were lodged in the presumed antiquity of their race or cultural forebearers.

In the center of all this vying for cultural antiquity to justify the supremacy of cultural doctrines, we now throw in the formulators of the Old Testament and the alleged origin of the Hebrews. They outdid all these other claims for antiquity of race and claimed lineage back to the very first man and woman ever created! With the garden of Eden story, they trumped every claim to cultural antiquity by every other people or culture in the surrounding regions. Even the ancient Egyptians couldn't trace back to the first humans created in any of their religious mythology. Thus, the Bible composers, with that one single story about Adam and Eve trumped every claim to racial antiquity by all other races and cultures.

From this claim, the Bible authors were then able to steal stories from other cultures, mostly Sumerian, change the names of the characters and make them all part of this hoary and non-existent Hebrew history. The Sumerian Utnapishtim became the biblical Noah with the new variant of the flood story. With the discovery of the clay Sumerian and Akkadian cuneiform tablets, the cultural appropriation folded into the Old Testament stories was finally revealed.

When the field of archaeology was in its infancy and explorers started researching into Egypt, their primary focus was to find the unnamed Pharaoh responsible for the fictitious Exodus. From its outset archaeology was focused on trying to prove the stores fabricated in the Bible. To date, this has not been accomplished. Excavations in Israel to this day support that Israel was just as pagan in its worship practices as the surrounding territories. With the unearthing of the Hittite cities, more tablets came to light that exposed the biblical myth for what it was. Except for those who are utterly blinded by their faith and the demand that these stories be truthful, the archaeological evidence is extremely sparse.

The Old Testament Hebrew history is like the novel *Gone with the Wind*. Yes, there was a Civil War. Yes, Atlanta burned.

No, there was no Rhett Butler or Scarlett O'Hara. Just as *Gone with the Wind* was a fiction wrapped around certain real events, it is still a fictional story, no different than the Bible. Yes, Ur of the Chaldees existed as an ancient Sumerian city. Yes, the Hittites existed. Yes, there were loads of Egyptian Pharaohs, but no, there was no shining Hebrew civilization, no Exodus as the story is told and little to no evidence of an organized Hebrew religious order as told in the Old Testament. There are clues that provide some foundation about the existence of some people referred to in Egyptian records as the Apiru, Habiru or Hapiru (Hebrew), but these were a group of caravan bandits that often raided the Egyptian trade caravans. They were vagabonds and raiders, and their existence is historically verifiable from Egyptian records. The Habiru did not have any formalized city organizations and were probably a bunch of thieving camel drivers.

The only thing that remotely resembles the biblical Exodus and fits roughly into the accepted time frame is the Egyptian expulsion of the Hyksos 'shepherd kings' who were Semitic and looted Egypt with their roughly 280-year reign in their capital city Avaris. The Egyptians finally got tired enough of their tyranny that they chased them out of Egypt into the area we know as Israel today. With these two stories we can see an utter inversion of history. With all these patently mythological events and the cultural appropriation of stories from other cultures and acknowledging that other civilizations, like the Hittites, actually existed, then we see the framework for the composition for the false Hebrew history which the entire Western world, through Christianity, has used as the measure of its historical accounting.

Just as Nietzsche observed in the opening passage to this chapter, all western knowledge is built on the ignorance and acceptance of this Hebrew mythology as fact.

As noted in my *WANA - Parts 1& 2,* outside the writings of the alleged Jewish historian, Josephus, who was a vassal to the Roman emperor, there is no evidence that has been found to date that supports this mythical Hebrew history. Josephus verifies the Old Testament and the Old Testament verifies Josephus, who was a self-admitted Essene. These are the only sources that verify the Hebrew mythology in totality. I asserted, and still stand by that assertion, that the Dead Sea Scrolls are the origin of the Old Testament. If the community at Qumran where the caves with the Dead Sea Scrolls were discovered was in fact an Essene community, which is still in contention, and Josephus was a self-admitted Essene, then the alleged historical noose closes even tighter around the neck of the perpetrators of the biblical fraud. Scholars who are only seeking the truth out of these mythological stories are being forced to reach the conclusion that the people of ancient Israel never reached any type of high civilization but were at best only tribal settlements. They built no grand cities, no Solomon's Temple or any of the other fanciful stories told in the Old Testament.

There is evidence from Babylonian records that tell about some people from Israel, or at least that region, being taken into captivity for a period of time and ultimately being released, but even then the Bible story doesn't completely cross-foot with the accounting from other surrounding cultures.

From this mythology we find the tenuous springboard that leads to the mythical character of Jesus, who was allegedly of the line of the biblical King David, of which any records about whose existence are virtually non-existent. If you read the New Testament, there are two separate lineages for Jesus that do not match each other, and over which Christians have tried to rationalize for centuries. Alternative Jewish origin stories do not match the Nativity story, claiming that Jesus' mother was a prostitute and his parentage was questionable, with some stories calling him the son of a Roman soldier and referring to him as the son of Pantera. Christians naturally protest these stories as hateful frauds because it busts the bubble of their mystical messiah. The truth is that Immanuel's mother did work as a temple prostitute who catered to high-class clientele. His parentage was unknown, and he also had a twin brother, James, against whom there was supreme sibling rivalry.

All of the stories fabricated in the New Testament about Jesus and his alleged divine birth are total fabrications and mirror other stories of divine birth that can be found in other cultures who had their mystical religion creators, like the Roman Mithras. Within the cultural milieu of the time, and preceding the formation of Christianity by centuries, stories of divine births were pretty standard. It only takes some historical research with the blinders of faith removed from one's eyes to find all this evidence. I am making no claims that can't be easily verified.

As for Yahweh, there was a minor Egyptian god associated with the moon named Yah, Iah or Aah. For a quick study (less than 5 mins.), I am providing a link to a YouTube video entitled *Yah the Egyptian Moon God vs. Yahweh.*

https://www.youtube.com/watch?v=eZbhXKMhEhY

A little review about Yahweh from Wikipedia under *Yahweh* might bring further light to this subject.

"Yahweh was the national god of the Iron Age kingdoms of Israel (Samaria) and Judah. His exact origins are disputed, although they reach back to the early Iron Age and even the Late Bronze: his name may have begun as an epithet of El, head of the Bronze Age Canaanite pantheon, **but the earliest plausible mentions of Yahweh are in ancient Egyptian texts that refer to a similar-sounding place name associated with the Shasu nomads of the southern Transjordan.** *Some scholars believe that Yahweh was originally thought to be one of the seventy sons of El, who later killed his siblings and displaced his father El at the head of the Israelite pantheon.*

In the oldest biblical literature, Yahweh is a typical ancient Near Eastern "divine warrior", who leads the heavenly army against Israel's enemies; he later became the main god of the Kingdom of Israel (Samaria) and of Judah, and *over time the royal court and Temple in Jerusalem promoted Yahweh as the god of the entire cosmos, possessing all the positive qualities previously attributed to the other gods and goddesses*. *By the end of the Babylonian captivity (6th century BCE), the very existence of foreign gods was denied, and* **Yahweh was proclaimed as the creator of the cosmos and the true god of all the world.***"

[Bold emphasis mine]

With these passages I hope you see the emergence of a pattern. Just as the Bible composers usurped all claims to ancient heritage by fabricating the Adam and Eve story in Genesis, the followers of the regional Egyptian god Yah or Iah, eventually altered the composition of this god to the creator of the entire universe.

I illustrated in *Gutting Mysticism* how the religion of the Egyptian Gnostics was a combination of goddess worship (Sophia) mixed with hive doctrines. In the Gnostic writings, it is the false god Ialdabaoth against whom the Gnostic gospels level their worst criticisms as being a mad god who is deluded with his power thinking he is more powerful than he is, etc. Given the goddess/hive orientation of the Gnostic writings and given what I have shared in my works about the war between Enki and Ninhursag, then there should be little doubt that the minor Egyptian god Yah is the same as the Jewish Yahweh and the Gnostic Ialdabaoth. The pieces of the puzzle fit. Also, if we look at the nomadic Shasu who worshipped Yah, we can only wonder if the Shasu were either associated with or were in fact the Habiru banditti who raided the Pharaoh's caravans in the same region. I can't give a definitive answer to this, but it is a curious set of facts worth mentioning.

In reference to the Bible or any other ancient writings, what many people in the world today don't think about much is that it has always been the elite classes who controlled literacy. People in the ancient world of Jesus' time did not read the alleged Hebrew history because it had not yet been fabricated. Everyone except the elite intelligentsia was illiterate with the exception of certain merchant classes who had the capability to tally their profit ledgers. The rest of the population operated from oral traditions passed down in songs and stories told around campfires. Writing was reserved to the elite and educated classes. What this should tell you, putting your head into the minds of our ancestors, is that they had to take the word of the priestly authorities who had the capability to read and write. Modern perceptions about early Christians is that they sat around poring over the Gospels and studying the words of Jesus. Nothing could be further from the truth.

The only people reading, writing and formulating these doctrines were the elite educated classes themselves. The self-proclaimed Apostle Paul is said to have been a tentmaker and a tax collector. He also had Roman citizenship, which many Christian writers have agonized over. By professing it himself, Paul claimed to be related to the 'littlest Herod', which is indicative that he was associated with the House of Herod, vassal kings to the Roman Emperor. Given this familial association, then the source of Paul's Roman citizenship becomes apparent. He probably ran a business making tents for the Roman armies, but since the Jews in Israel at that time were close to the revolt of 70 AD, Paul's close association with the Romans doesn't fit the Jewish narrative, so it had to be whitewashed.

What has come down through the ages as Christianity has little to do with the psoyca teachings of Immanuel and are hinged upon the writings and teachings about the metaphysical Jesus character, which were all predicated on a vision I profess was delivered by a hive encounter when Saul/Paul was blinded for three days on the Road to Damascus. From that moment of ecstatic conversion, then the New Testament doctrines about the mystical Jesus started taking shape, with the Pauline letters being the seminal source of information that created what became Roman Catholicism. Just as Ninhursag and the hive wanted total universal conquest of this planet as elucidated in *Gutting Mysticism*, Catholic means universal. You should be able to put these pieces together to see the tapestry start to weave together. There have been more learned scholars than me who have seen that what is called Christianity is a far cry from the teachings of Immanuel and are in fact a mystical fraud perpetrated by the self-appointed Apostle Paul, who never knew Immanuel in his lifetime. Roman Catholicism is Paulianity, not Christianity, slathered with heavy doses of goddess worship through the divine Mother Mary. Like many other pagan traditions, the goddess worship of old was grafted wholesale into the tapestry of the new Roman state religion.

To become a person of knowledge requires that we often study the things we really don't want to. For myself, having to wade through Christian apologetics and the incessant arguments for and against Christianity was a requirement to be able to see through these stories. Most of us have a bad taste for the stiff-necked and rigid Christian culture that has mandated western behaviors for 1,700 years since Constantine formalized it as the Roman State religion and sought to expand Roman control worldwide. The Roman Senators of old, in many cases, simply changed their garments to those of the Roman Church and the Roman Empire continued under a different guise. The ancient religion of the alleged Hebrews has no association or similarity to New Testament Paulianity beyond the fabricated lineage of Jesus and the purported prophecies in the Old Testaments that allegedly foretold his coming as the Jewish messiah.

The Bible was written backward and forward at the same time, with those writing the religion for the gentiles in the New Testament and writing backward to create alleged prophecies that linked Old Testament and New Testament ideologies together. From the standpoint of religious ideologies, Judaism and Christianity are like oil and water, but in order to sell the false historical narrative of the Jews as the foundation of all history on the planet, the two systems of belief had to be joined together to cognitively bilk the masses into buying the lie. The pivot point in history is the composition of the Dead Sea Scrolls becoming the Old Testament, while many of the mystical doctrines of the Gnostics were melded into the New Testament coupled with Paul's new conversion stories about the divine Jesus, the messiah of all humanity. Prior to the discovery of the Dead Sea Scrolls there is no extant copy of the Old Testament or the alleged Hebrew history to be found anywhere on the planet, there are only *legends* that it existed. There is not one single jot of historical, archaeological or textual evidence that supports these legendary biblical claims outside Josephus.

The concepts of baptism and salvation of the soul find their origins in the cult of Isis, which was a stiff competitor to Christianity until it was finally quashed and driven underground. The salvation cult of Isis substantially predates the birth of Jesus. The doctrine of Plato's divine Monad was the launching point for what later became the ideology of both Judaism and Christianity with the single God who created the whole universe. As other scholars have observed, Christianity is Platonism matured. I hate reading the meanderings of philosophers of any age. They are too full of their own self-importance to make their writings in the least palatable.

It is from the ancient Greek philosophers that all academia and its practices grew. It is a realm of self-congratulatory egos all too full of themselves and their presumed knowledge to not warrant a certain amount of disdain. Yet I also had to force myself to read as much of what I could stand to digest to reach the conclusions I have in the books I have written. One will never advance their consciousness very far only feeding our minds with things that serve our limited self-interests. One will never develop a 360° perception of the world so long as we insist on only looking at a sliver of the reality that surrounds us and confirms our belief biases.

Those who would most vehemently protest what I write here and in my other works are those who have cognitive turf to protect. They have their world built on beliefs and tunnel vision perceptions and they all have something to defend – their perceptual *reality*. When you build all your knowledge on a foundation of ignorance, no matter how educated you think you are, then you are only professing self-important ignorance masquerading itself as knowledge. Academia is as closed a cognitive box as that of any religion believer. There are those in academia who raise very relevant questions, but even they have turf to protect once their minds are made up about their theories and conclusions.

5. Dark History of Humanity

I am going to open this chapter with some observations of Friedrich Nietzsche from one of his lesser known works, *Untimely Meditations*. What follows is from meditation number 2, *"On the Uses and Disadvantages of History for Life"*:

"'In any case, I hate everything that merely instructs me without augmenting or directly invigorating my activity.' These words are from Goethe, and they may stand as a sincere at the ceterum cense beginning of our meditation on the value of history. For its intention is to show why instruction without invigoration, why knowledge not attended by action, why history as a costly superfluity and luxury, must, to use Goethe's word, be seriously hated by us - hated because we still lack even the things we need and the superfluous is the enemy of the necessary. We need history, certainly, but we need it for reasons different from those for which the idler in the garden of knowledge needs it, even though he may look nobly down on our rough and charmless needs and requirements. We need it, that is to say, for the sake

of life and action, not so as to turn comfortably away from life and action, let alone for the purpose of extenuating the self seeking life and the base and cowardly action. We want to serve history only to the extent that history serves life: for it is possible to value the study of history to such a degree that life becomes stunted and degenerate - a phenomenon we are now forced to acknowledge, painful though this may be, in the face of certain striking symptoms of our age."

"This meditation too is untimely, because I am here attempting to look afresh at something of which our time is rightly proud – its cultivation of history -- as being injurious to it, a defect and deficiency in it; because I believe, indeed, that we are all suffering from a consuming fever of history and ought at least to recognize that we are suffering from it. But if Goethe was right to assert that when we cultivate our virtues we at the same time cultivate our faults, and if, as everyone knows, a hypertrophied virtue such as the historical sense of our age appears to be - can ruin a nation just as effectively as a hypertrophied vice: then there can be no harm in indulging me for this once."

"Consider the cattle, grazing as they pass you by: they do not know what is meant by

yesterday or today, they leap about, eat, rest, digest, leap about again, and so from morn till night and from day to day, fettered to the moment and its pleasure or displeasure, and thus neither melancholy nor bored. This is a hard sight for man to see; for, though he thinks himself better than the animals because he is human, he cannot help envying them their happiness - what they have, a life neither bored nor painful, is precisely what he wants, yet he cannot have it because he refuses to be like an animal. A human being may well ask an animal: 'Why do you not speak to me of your happiness but only stand and gaze at me?' The animal would like to answer, and say: 'The reason is I always forget what I was going to say' - but then he forgot this answer too, and stayed silent: so that the human being was left wondering.

But he also wonders at himself, that he cannot learn to forget but clings relentlessly to the past: however far and fast he may run, this chain runs with him. *And it is a matter for wonder: a moment, now here and then gone, nothing before it came, again nothing after it has gone, nonetheless returns as a ghost and disturbs the peace of a later moment. A leaf flutters from the scroll of time, floats away – and suddenly floats back again and falls into the man's lap. Then the man says 'I remember' and envies the animal, who* *at once forgets and for whom every moment really dies, sinks back into night and fog and is extinguished forever. Thus the animal lives unhistorically: for it is contained in the present, like a number without any awkward fraction left over; it does not know how to dissimulate, it conceals nothing and at every instant appears wholly as what it is; it can therefore never be anything but honest. Man, on the other hand, braces himself against the great and ever greater pressure of what is past: it pushes him down or bends him sideways, it encumbers his steps as a dark, invisible burden which he can sometimes appear to disown and which in traffic with his fellow men he is only too glad to disown so as to excite their envy. That is why it affects him like a vision of a lost paradise to see the herds grazing or, in closer proximity to him, a child which, having as yet nothing of the past to shake off, plays in blissful blindness between the hedges of past and future Yet its play must be disturbed; all too soon it will be called out of its state of forgetfulness. Then it will learn to understand the phrase 'it was': that password which gives conflict, suffering and satiety access to man so as to remind him what his existence fundamentally is - an imperfect tense that can never become a perfect one. If death at last brings the desired forgetting, by that act it at the same time extinguishes the present and all existence and therewith sets the seal on the knowledge that existence is only an uninterrupted has-been, a thing that lives by negating, consuming and contradicting itself."*

[Bold emphasis mine]

The last chapter should fully illustrate the burden of a false history that humanity insists on embracing. As Nietzsche observes, the past just continues to build and we carry it around like a ball and chain. I will provide explanations in a later chapter about why we have this ball and chain. This past we carry around, however, is rarely learned from and people crave to return to some misperceived paradisiacal world of the past that never existed. We can't live in the present without these yearnings for a mythical past where we have convinced ourselves that things were better and easier for our ancestors – the lost Golden Age. Humanity can't move forward because of its perpetual insistence to return to this non-existent mythical past. When all our presumed history is built upon a fabricated foundation of fraud, as illustrated in the last chapter, we then become slaves to a whitewashed and fraudulent history. This book is here to set the record straight about our presumed idyllic past and cast the history of the human species on this planet in the correct and dismal light that truly was. You better have a strong stomach to face this past, because whether you choose to believe it or not in the face of your perceptual illusions based on fraudulent history, it is our origins.

From here forward, the information is going to get deep and ugly. There have been several books published that present humans being created as a slave race to offworld gods. Zechariah Sitchin's stories, adapted from Sumerian, Akkadian and Babylonian cuneiform tablets and the stories about the Anunnaki gods tell us this story. William Bramley also covered this in his 1989 book, *The Gods of Eden*, as did Michael Tellinger in his book, *Slave Species to the Gods: The Secret History of the Anunnaki and Their Mission on Earth*. Whether anyone wants to read these books is left to their own prerogative. I have read (and studied) all of Sitchin's work since the 70's when *The Twelfth Planet* appeared in the marketplace. I have also read Bramley's book. I have not read the Tellinger book, but by the title you can tell it is just more Anunnaki rehash initiated by Sitchin with perhaps a minor interpretive spin on it. I only bring these books to your attention to back my own claims about humanity being created as a slave race to offworld gods, and I use the term gods very loosely in all these contexts. I have yet to find any author who has done the investigative work that I presented in the *WANA* series of books that zeroes in on the race of interstellar conquerors we call the Orioners, although I think I have presented substantial evidence about their existence from historical mythology.

The stories that follow are how things were. They are going to be very grim and that is intentional, for without understanding humanity's grim and tragic past as a species, you can't comprehend why we are as screwed up a species as we are today. As you read these stories, I am inviting you to try and get your mind into the heads of our ancestors who experienced these things. Don't just read this information as if it is just a science fiction or horror tale that you only grasp on a superficial level of your intellect like reading a novel. To read these stories with that level of perception you will never understand what humanity has been subjected to throughout its history. If you want pragmatic psoyca advanced awareness you have to *see* and *know* the whole truth. Superficially intellectualizing these revelations will not give you the pragmatic and sobering knowledge required for ownership and personal responsibility as a fully functional human being. I make no excuses for the graphic nature of these stories. It is humanity's past in synopsized form, ugly as it is.

The Orioner race were master genetic manipulators. They had totally conquered the physical genetic code and had gone even deeper into some knowledge on the sub-genetic or energetic level. This will be explained as we move forward. I don't recall whether I have shared that information in any of my books to date, but it will be revealed in this volume to show you the magnitude of their tyrannical plans for the multiverse.

People have a rather sanitized view of slavery with the enslavement of Blacks in southern America as their leading example. I am in no way justifying slavery of any nature, but I am going to put things in context here that casts some truthful light onto a highly propagandized emotional issue. For all those that used slavery in the U.S., their slaves were a financial investment. Yes, they were considered property as slaves have always been considered throughout history, and many of the slaves experienced terrible circumstances like having their children ripped away and sold to other slaveowners. Through a lot of propaganda, starting with the Abolitionist movement that led to the U.S. Civil War, it is the very worst aspects of slavery that permeates the public imagination – stories of brutal slave masters whipping their slaves for certain offenses, killing runaway slaves, etc. What gets overlooked is the fact that most slaveowners didn't abuse their slaves as much as the public believes.

To a slave holder, their slaves were their means to production. If the slaves were abused, not fed, or uselessly beaten, then they couldn't work the fields to harvest the products that the owner had to get to market and sell to support their business venture. Cotton planters are the most well-known type of slaveholders because that was a primary industry that the Southern plantation owners used to sell to Northern textile industries. As such, the slaves were a necessary element to keep Southern businesses functioning. This being so, then to beat all your slaves as the Hollywood industry and Abolitionists of an earlier age would have us believe would mean that your livelihood would come to a swift end. Many of the slave traders were Northern Jews. The Jews often played a seminal role in the slave trade. This is one aspect of the slave trade that is not discussed much in American historical context, but which can be easily verified with a little diligent research on the internet.

Having shared all this, the slavery that occurred in the South is the measuring stick of how people perceive slavery today. The people that write the books about being slaves to alien races, I have little doubt, are using this measuring stick to formulate their ideas about the slavery imposed on humanity by their offworld overlords. In this respect, they are viewing slavery with a Pollyanna perspective.

The Orioners abused races across the cosmos. They were even more abusive of their genetic creations than they were the races they conquered, and they did not treat these conquered races kindly at all. Since the Orioners could produce as many slave races of many varieties and specialized hybridized species, their creations were property in the truest sense of the word. They had no Abolitionists or anyone else who could stand against them in what they did with their property. They were immoral and basically conscienceless psychopaths. When they created the Earth human species, if the stories left to us can be believed, at the behest of the Anunnaki, they were designed to pick up the labor gap that the Anunnaki protesting workers were providing. As I explained in the *WANA* books, humans were two-legged cattle to the Orioners and all subsequent races that tampered with our genetics. There are races out there who were once here that still refer to humanity on this planet as cattle.

Under Orioner overlordship, their human cattle were rarely provided shelter and their food rations were minimal. Humans slept in the open on the ground, and it is probable that they weren't even provided hay on which to sleep. They were animals and they were treated like animals. Our ancestors worked forced labor until they dropped. Most did not live past the age of 20 before they were literally worked to death and disposed of. The Orioners also used their two-legged cattle as a mainstay of their dinner table, having tired of the unpleasant taste of the Anunnaki. Our ancestors were cattle in every sense of the word. Get your head around that in earnest, don't just take this as a fanciful story. It is from these subliminal memories implanted into our psyche by the hapiym virus that we have such a dread of offworld aliens attacking us and eating us.

I related the story that after the Sirius B incident that this planet had been subsequently terraformed by other alien races. When the Orioners finally claimed this planet, it was a worldwide wilderness. When they 'colonized' this planet, there was probably not much here regarding the multitudes of lifeforms that we are presently aware of. There were no wild cattle or pigs, nor most of the other wildlife we have come to take as an evolutionary standard. Many of these species were introduced to this planet much later by other races who transported them from their own home worlds. That being so, then the human cattle became the go-to meat supplement for both the Orioners as well as the Anunnaki.

As certain necessary outposts and edifices were built on this vast planetary wilderness, eventually some of these humans did wind up housed in barn-like structures but still probably slept on the ground. All the myths produced by Darwinist theory are merely wishful thinking. There was no evolutionary rise of humans from apes as Darwin conjectured and modern science foolishly embraces. It was tens of thousands of years before the human condition progressed much beyond what is just described, and none of that advancement was brought about by the Orioners themselves. All they cared about was getting what work they wanted done by their cattle, and they were merciless in driving humanity to produce their desires. The casualty rate was not much a concern for those who could produce as many cloned workers as they desired to replace cattle shortfalls. They did not rely strictly on human breeding and the aging process to fulfill their labor requirements. Just as people will eat veal or leg of lamb because the meat is more tender, the same could be said of human babies and small children whose meat was more tender than the stringy muscular meat of overworked adult cattle. Is the gravity of this slavery starting to leak into your consciousness now? When we view slavery of this nature, then the slavery of blacks in the South becomes pretty genteel by comparison. I am not diminishing the lot of anyone held in bondage, but we have to view things from a realistic standpoint before we can understand why the human race on this planet was created.

Once human families started to develop, if a slave did anything to rankle one of their overlords, and I have little doubt the offenses were often minor, then these offenders would be given an example by being forced to watch these godly overlords eat their children or families in front of their eyes. Sometimes they would kill the offender as well after witnessing such a horror show. It was not only the Orioners who would set such examples, but also the Anunnaki and some of the other races they held in vassalage to them when they colonized the planet. There are some folks living in the cosmos who were here then, and it is from some of these contacts that we have been provided these stories. This is just part of the horror show of humanity's past, and because of the hive collective's memory, we all have these memories buried deep within us, what Jung called the collective unconscious.

We must ask why virtually all our stories about aliens have to do with monsters that invade from space and eat your face when they get here. These stories by varied science fiction and horror authors are part of the dredged-up memories of our ancient past passed onto us by the virus memory database. This is the basis for all these visceral fears in all of us. The hive collected the memories and experiences of those ancient human cattle hosts and it just continued with the memories with every new hive cell infection into its human host. Are you starting to see the magnitude of the overall horror of humanity's past? If you want to know why we are such a fearful species today, you only need to look at the buried subconscious memories that the mind virus infected us with to see this continuing horror in our modern world.

It wasn't known at the time that the Orioners claimed this planet, but Earth is a planet that can function with multiple frequencies as the same time. The Orioners were 8th dimensional beings. The Anunnaki were 4D beings. Humans are strictly 3D beings. Other races from the stars that later inhabited this planet originated from planets that operate at the 5D frequency (the Andromedans to name just one), and from 6D planets (the Arcturans) as well as those from varied frequencies such as the Norse gods who were 4D and some Pleiadian races who were 5D. Because Earth could function with all these frequencies operating at the same time, all these offworld races could interface together and with human cattle on this planet in a literal physical sense. This is how humans could interface with their gods.

There is a race of beings from the Cassiopeia constellation who had greater technological capabilities than even the Orioners, with their vast technological knowledge, couldn't conquer. This race became sort of like cosmic referees in the affairs of the other gods. In time, these referees had to step in when the abuse by the offworld gods got out of hand and the multidimensional gateway of this planet that allowed all this multidimensional interplay between Earth humans and their gods came to an end. This is when the physical gods 'disappeared' to humanity. Humanity was locked into a strictly 3D environment and they could no longer perceive their gods who came from higher dimensions, except for the Anunnaki and the infamous Greys, who were both low 4D frequency beings.

Dimensionally speaking, I have brought up the idea of 3D operating within a certain bandwidth similar to a radio dial. I referenced this in regard to raising one's vibration. Every dimensional frequency operates from similar bandwidths. Between the dimensions, as one transitions from one to another, say from 3D to 4D, there is like a crossover zone where one operating at a low 4D frequency can crossover and function in 3D. It is through this frequency overlap that the Anunnaki and the Greys were able to continue to interface with humans on this planet in 3D after that multidimensional access was shut down.

I explained in the *WANA* books about the wars between the gods that eventually led to closing this multidimensional gateway. The Cassiopeian referees, after continued warnings against what was happening on this planet, finally got a bellyful of the tyranny and closed the multidimensional interface. One day in some deep dark future if humanity survives itself, it may open up once again for more civil interfaces with stellar races. Because of these dimensional barriers, all the hype out there in the New

Age arena about aliens coming to save us should now be evidenced as even more ludicrous hogwash.

Even after the vacating of the gods, either being eliminated through warfare or just wandering back home from Earth on their own, the issue of slavery was always present. The Anunnaki were perhaps somewhat kinder masters than the Orioners, but the gods, just like humans, had their varieties of assholes. Some were 'good' gods, and some were merciless bloodthirsty tyrants. Gods like the ancient Moloch demanded human sacrifice as did numerous other known and unknown gods.

Aside from eating humans for food, both the Orioners and the Anunnaki fed off human emotional energy, as I reported in the *WANA* books. Making someone sacrifice their children, mostly under penalty of death for non-adherence to the sacrificial rites, produced a tremendous amount of terror energy for these beastly gods to feed upon. As I reported in *WANA – Part 1*, the Anunnaki figured out that humans emitted a variety of emotional energies and started feeding on those whereas the Orioners were solely focused on feeding on the energies of fear and outright terror. Coupled with feeding on these energies, these gods could harvest and then store them, after which they could use those stolen energies to create their own energetic programs, or what was anciently known as magic spells.

Before the gods all disappeared, the Aryans invaded Earth. The Aryans, although representative of all the human races that existed on that planet at that time, were created from original genetic stock from races who live in the stars. When the Orioners 'invited' the other races they had conquered to participate in this

Earth endeavor, they told them they could do anything they wanted to with the human genetic stock, but they could only use the human genetic template which the Orioners themselves created and provided as genetic fodder for experimentation. Because of this mandate, when Ninhursag created her Aryan armies, she didn't trust the Orioner human template, wisely figuring out that there were hidden hooks in the genetics supplied by the Orioner human template. Therefore, she attained the genetic material from the races that already existed out there to fabricate her Aryan armies into being in her own laboratories on Nibiru. These Aryan creations are who have run the planet by proxy since their arrival around 3760 BC. They are the global elite.

Under the rule of these invading tyrants, human slavery continued. In ancient Rome, for instance, not only were slaves considered chattel property, but everyone in a patriarch's household was up for sale or death if they didn't fulfill the household master's mandates. They could sell their wives and often sold their children into slavery for familial offenses. The lot of the slave was even worse. When the Romans conquered territories, or any other Aryan tyrant for that matter, those they didn't kill in battle and raiding were automatically doomed to slavery. This included men, women and children. With such an abundance of slaves generated through conquest, the marketplace for slaves was a booming business.

Many slaveholders created brothels and made their slaves prostitutes, which was legal in ancient Rome as a legitimate business practice. Many temples had slaves dedicated to them for similar purposes. Prostituting slaves was not just limited to women, but also included men and although not widely reported, children to cater to the needs of pedophiles. In many cases, sexual abuse of slaves in the household had a blind eye turned to it publicly because slaves were no more than furniture. If the slaveowner had an eye to sexually abuse any slave, then there was no law to protect the slaves and no law that said the owner couldn't take any liberty with his property that he chose.

Rich Romans would often put on gala events where they paraded out their slaves for the sexual consumption by their guests. Slaves were also used in gladiatorial endeavors as moneymaking enterprises. The slave could either go into the arena and fight to the death or they could face death for refusing to do so. Because of 'Christian sensibilities' this graphic sexual nature of ancient slavery is swept under the rug, and when someone tells people about it, they are unwilling to believe this sordid truth.

Based on one verse in Leviticus where Christians and Jews are told that man shall not lie with man, the stigma of homosexuality has haunted gays and lesbians for centuries. Even in the patriarchal society of ancient Rome, homosexuality was not spurned unless a patriarch held the submissive position in a male on male relationship. So long as the patriarch was the penetrator instead of the penetrated, then homosexual engagements were accepted in Roman society. In both Greece and Rome, slaveowners or sponsors would have catamites, boys who were used for homosexual purposes. Have no doubt that little girls were not equally sexually abused in those cultures as well. This is the ugly past that Christianity in the west has whitewashed from the pages of history and created such a sexually neurotic culture. Even today in India, families sell their daughters for the practice of temple prostitution, so the institution has not died out. It is only in the domesticated western mind that such things are intolerable. Again, I am not justifying slavery or what it has brought to the world, but until one understands the true tyranny of the slavery of old, the recent episodes of slavery pale in comparison.

Through all of these episodes, the hive infected human hosts have carried these memories on an unconscious level. The hive plugged in all this 'knowledge' when it infected us. It may be buried deep within our cellular memory landscape, but have no doubt that these nagging memories lie within all of us.

Since there is no God and no judgment day, and the Aryans are intimately aware of this fact, then you should find an understanding for why the elite like the Jeffrey Epsteins of the world continue to do what they do to tyrannize and control their human cattle. Where Christian moralists find many of those ancient practices abhorrent and sinful, most of their own unwillingness to ponder their own sexual desires is out of fear of divine retribution. I am not here to dictate to anyone what their moral stance should or shouldn't be, but the sexual repression instilled by Christian thinking has turned us away from our humanity and traded it for divine promises, reinforced through the concept of sin and the fear of eternal damnation. You can thank the hive virus for these false doctrines of the divine. Friedrich Nietzsche spared no amount of scorn for these practices and he was very thorough in his polemic against them in *The Anti-Christ*.

6. The Tyranny of Ninhursag and the Hive

I am going to focus on Ninhursag in this chapter more than the tyranny of Enki, because the tyranny of Enki is exhibited in the practices of the Old Testament. He was neurotic, vengeful and murderous when he didn't get his own way. He advocated wholesale slaughter and land theft as well as slavery. The Christian world is a reflection of his mind.

In the war between Ninhursag and Enki, sex became a seminal weapon. Where Enki wanted to suppress all human sexual desires and mandated that they only be used for reproduction, Ninhursag saw human sexual desires as a means to exploit human energies to gather more power to herself. Many of the most popular goddess cults of the ancient world professed drunkenness and sexual revelry. The cults of the gods Dionysus and Bacchus are exemplary examples of such cults reveling in abandon with sexual orgies in the sacred groves of the goddess being a pinnacle act of the ecstatic rituals associated with these cults. This is one reason Enki demanded that the groves of the goddess be cut down and the wood burned in the Old Testament.

In the ancient pagan world, in the cults associated with Ninhursag in her many and varied roles as either god or goddess, you will find tremendous overtones of sexuality. The licentious god Pan was associated with her rituals, as was the god Priapus, who was a god with a gigantic penis. The symbol of Priapus was the erect phallus, and it was only with the unearthing of Pompei from the ashes of Vesuvius that these things came to light. The Roman church over the centuries had systematically removed similar statuary throughout the Roman Empire, and as a result of this intentional expunging of evidence, the modern world had no real knowledge about the sexual cults and practices across the ancient world. When Vesuvius buried Pompei in its ashes, it created a time capsule from 79 AD and the Roman world. What had been expunged and removed from all other edifices in the Roman world, was captured *in situ* in Pompei. Pompei was not the exception in the Roman world as some would have you believe but was a prime example of the ancient Roman Empire.

In Pompei they unearthed a wealth of erotic art in mosaic form, erotic paintings on walls in private dwellings, statues to Priapus and even the hovel houses of prostitution in which the prostitutes plied their trade. If you want to understand the ancient Roman Empire and its sexual practices, just do some research into Pompei. Our modern Christianized and tampered-with history would lead you to believe otherwise, but Pompei opens a window into the past and illustrates what a key role sex and sexuality played in that world. In today's world all of that has been historically suppressed and we only get a sanitized and very distorted view of history.

There is no point of exact origin for the sexual cults of the ancient world, but there is evidence of them being in place for thousands of years, starting with the goddess Inanna, the Sumerian goddess of lust and fertility. There are two stories about Inanna, stories about the original Inanna and then the Ninhursag overlay stories. When Inanna changed her character from a warrior goddess and became a goddess of lust was when Ninhursag stole the identity of the original Inanna and set herself up to steal anything associated with the original Inanna, no different than Ninhursag later did with the goddess Isis and others. Nin was also big on peddling herself as the virgin Mother goddess. Few have understood this virgin motherhood mythology, so I will explain it now, if I haven't covered it in my other works.

Ninhursag was a hermaphrodite and may have not had the capability to breed children. I won't claim this is a definitive fact, but only as conjecture. But where the virgin mother myth finds its roots lies in the fact that she was an expert in genetics. Just like the Orioners, she could 'give birth' to many creatures, and she did. In this regard, she was the 'mother' of these creations without having to give birth herself. This is the origin and meaning to all virgin mother myths that come from the ancient world – an enigmatic supernatural mystery solved with a pragmatic explanation.

Ninhursag knew all about the human sexual desires as did Enki. Where Enki sought to repress these desires so he could feed on the energies of guilt and shame produced by his doctrines of sin, Nin chose instead to capitalize on these human desires and push them to the extreme, thereby harvesting all the love and devotion from the followers of her cults, whether as Dionysus, Demeter, Cybele or any other god/goddess cult that invited sexual abandon and revelry. She catered fully to these natural human desires. What people don't realize about energetic magic is that power willingly given away is more powerful than energy stolen. Nin preyed on these human desires by promoting them in her cults and people accepted these tenets of worship with open arms and rampant desire. Ninhursag fed on all of it, the energies produced by sexual unions performed in rituals honoring her as well as the love and devotion of these followers for being given the chance to exercise their human desires without scorn, guilt or shame.

I am firmly convinced that the patriarchal nature of the ancient world was handed down by the misogynistic Orioners. When Enki was appointed as lord of the Earth (En-Ki) and removed from his position of leadership on Nibiru as lord of the watery abyss (E-A), the Orioners also gave him the energetic spellwork to keep the patriarchal system in place. Whatever this spellwork was, no matter how much Ninhursag tried to overcome Enki's rule and conquer humanity for her own purposes, this Orioner spellwork was Enki's hole card to play whenever Nin and her devious plans got to be too troublesome. No matter what Nin tried, Enki always held that Orioner trump card to stop her in her tracks.

Although Enki was a decent magician in his own right, he never possessed the same genius that Nin exhibited. From our external sources who knew her, and one who worked intimately with her for thousands of years, she was probably one of the most skilled magical adepts that ever lived. She was also one of the most dangerous creatures every created. She was creative and innovative beyond imagination in what she could do with her inventiveness and magical abilities. Sadly, she used all this talent for the gathering of power and vainglory.

In Greek mythology and religion, we find a number of instances of revered gynomorphs. On Wikipedia under *Gynomorph* we find the following:

> *"In Greek mythology and religion, a gynomorph was a bi-gendered god with both masculine and feminine characteristics. Gynomorphs were portrayed as effeminate young males, like Dionysos, a masculine god who possessed distinctly feminine features. Gynomorphs retained the creative capacity of female divinities, they had cosmic wombs, but they also possessed the inseminating abilities attributed to male divinities."*

This description is referenced on Wikipedia from D.C.A Hillman's book, *Hermaphrodites, Gynomorphs and Jesus.* After reading some of Hillman's work, I have reached the conclusion that his particular bias is anti-Roman Church and leans more toward the mystical preferences of Neoplatonism and modern Transpersonal Psychology favoring the doctrines of Ninhursag. Despite this bias, Hillman missed the boat in his discussion on gynomorphs. He did not take into consideration a physical hermaphrodite creature like Ninhursag playing the roles of both god and goddess in the ancient cults she created to win and hold favor of her human herds. Hillman found gynomorphs, like the mixed god Hermaphroditus (a blend of the god Hermes and Aphrodite as I have presented in other works), fascinating enough subjects to write a book about them, but there is nothing in his book that reflects the true nature of why gynomorphic gods and why the cult worship of such creatures weas pushed in the ancient world. Without the knowledge or consideration of a physical hermaphrodite god/goddess like Ninhursag driving such an agenda, the fascination with them in Greek religion goes unexplained.

Although possessing the sex organs of both male and female, her preference was for her female side except where it came to harnessing power through playing the role of a male god. Nin was the first gender bender in these ancient cults. She pushed homosexuality and role mixing between men and women in her rituals. It is her doctrines that produced the loosening of these rigid gender classifications in her religions and cults, often having her male priests dress as women, and in the case of the Galli priests, the priests of the cult of Cybele, they would castrate themselves in exhibitions of public ecstasy, then run through the town holding their genitals aloft like a trophy for their dedication to this great mother goddess. Such actions are recorded in Roman history.

In Greek Athens, a city dedicated to the goddess Athena, we find the first whispers of feminism in the ancient past to challenge the misogynistic system of patriarchy handed down from the Orioners. We also find the gynomorphs introduced into Greek religion, and of course, temple prostitution. Homosexuality was readily accepted in ancient Greece which is why to this day sodomy is referred to as Greek. Initially the Romans hated the importation of Eastern cultures like those of the Greeks, especially under the rule of the Emperor Augustus, who did everything he could to legislate morality on his watch. After decades of his rule and his death, things took a sharp turn with the rise of the Emperor Tiberius, who was purportedly a follower of the Isis cult. In his later years Tiberius was a lecher and he personally curried Caligula with his sexual depravities while raising him and basically holding him captive on the Isle of Capri. Caligula also built temples to Isis during his short reign before his corruption and depravities led to his being murdered by his own personal guards.

The goddess cults were also supreme in other areas of the East like Israel, regardless of how the Bible authors tried to alter history to mask this truth. The Jews in Israel worshipped Ninhursag in her role as Ashtoreth or Astarte, also known as Ishtar in Babylon. In all these regions where her cults took shape we find drugs, drunkenness and sexual revelry taking place in her sacred groves. Temple prostitution was also a mainstay in her cults with priests often acting as pimps to the temple whores. In the Eleusinian Mystery cult that worshipped the goddess Demeter and the annual return of her daughter Persephone from the underworld, the ceremonial revelry started with a drink called *kykeon*, allegedly brewed from barley which produced visionary psychedelic ecstasies. There is some suggestion that the psychedelic properties of *kykeon* were produced by the hallucinogen ergot, which is a mold that develops on rye and other cereals. The recipe for *kykeon* remains a mystery to this day, and the ergot mold is the best speculation on what caused the hallucinogenic religious ecstasies from drinking the concoction which was reserved for the celebrations of Demeter and the ritual pilgrimage to her temple, where her followers also sought visions provided by the goddess. Regarding these mysteries, Wikipedia informs us in part under *Eleusinian Mysteries*:

> *"The rites, ceremonies, and beliefs were kept secret and consistently preserved from antiquity. For the initiated, the rebirth of Persephone symbolized the eternity of life which flows from generation to generation, **and they believed that they would have a reward in the afterlife**. There are many paintings and pieces of pottery that depict various aspects of the Mysteries. Since **the Mysteries involved visions and conjuring of an afterlife,** some scholars believe that the power and longevity of the Eleusinian Mysteries, a consistent set of rites, ceremonies and experiences that spanned two millennia, came from psychedelic drugs. The name of the town, Eleusís, seems to be Pre-Greek and it is probably a counterpart with Elysium and the goddess Eileithyia."*

> [Bold emphasis mine]

When we look up *Eileithyia* on Wikipedia we discover:

> *"Eileithyia or Ilithyia was the Greek goddess of childbirth and midwifery. In the cave of Amnisos (Crete) she was related **with the annual***

__birth of the divine child__, and her cult is connected with Enesidaon (the earth shaker), who was the chthonic aspect of the god Poseidon. It is possible that her cult is related with the cult of Eleusis. In his Seventh Nemean Ode, Pindar refers to her as the maid to or seated beside the Moirai (Fates) and responsible for creating offspring."

[Bold emphasis mine]

From these passages we find the beginning echoes of the Christian heaven and the divine child Jesus of later Christian mythology, and perhaps now you can understand why Hillman linked gynomorphs to Jesus in his book. Jesus is not the first divine child that existed in the ancient world. He was only one of many predecessors, whether Christians want to accept this or not.

If one looks at the current political spectrum with an alleged 63 different genders, transsexuals, transgenders, revolutionary feminism and gay pride in light of this ancient conflict between Enki and Ninhursag, the ancient battle for controlling human consciousness using sexuality as a weapon is still being waged hammer and tong today. With no concept of history or the information shared in my books, the world is clueless about Ninhursag's revolutionary nature and the war between the gods using human sexuality as one of the premier weapons to fight that ongoing war. These two ancient gods are dead and gone, but here is the other factor that needs consideration in this equation, and that is the infection of the hapiym virus.

I have written extensively about how the virus created its false persona we think of as our ego. The virus was a recording device, a massive database which all hive cells were linked into. I am going to do my best to explain this where it is comprehensible, and I ask you to really work hard to get your head around these concepts because they have tremendous ramifications. Because the hive collective was one massive cosmic database of information, a collective of all the memories of every human life ever lived, every hive cell carried these memories when they infected us. As the individual hive cells took over our minds and our physiology, these memories were embedded into our cellular memory on a deep unconscious level. This is what Carl Jung called the collective unconscious without ever realizing it was a result of the shared memory database of the hapiym hive collective embedded in all humanity by the virus. Whether we have these memories on a conscious level or not, we still carry these memories buried deep inside us. Because of the nature of the war between Enki and Ninhursag and their using our sexuality against us, we all carry inner trepidations about sex as a result of this virus infection.

I explained in *Gutting Mysticism* Nin's plan to take over all humanity through the aegis of her elevating herself to the hive in the role as the Queen of Heaven. If we look at the current Marxist Globalist revolutionary atmosphere and the amount of sexual disfunction present in the political arena, one can't help but wonder whether she used her control of the local human hive consortium to plug programs into people's bodymind physiology to create and reinvigorate this battlefield. I won't assert that this is what occurred but given the nature of how the hive virus could program our human forms and minds to its will, I think it is a point that bears consideration, as 'out there' as the idea may be.

One thing is certain, the gender confused segment of our culture seems to have exploded in a very short period of time, which bears consideration for that reason if no other. I'm not talking about homosexuals who have been a part of humanity for untold ages, but the other segments of transgenders and multiple gender claimants who seemingly appeared out of nowhere without any historical record of their existence in the past. I don't think it can all be attributed to the educational indoctrination system or simple psychological manipulation, which the Fabian Marxists have been in control of for decades. This is what leads me to examine the whole phenomenon as having a more significant and hidden basis, such as hive cell manipulation as a cause for it. Given Nin's nature and her desire for ultimate conquest over humanity, remaking the world in her own sexually neurotic image would lend credence to such an idea. The greater reality is stranger than our limited perception of the first cognition illusion in which we live. Given Nin's avaricious quest for power and her tyrannical bent, I wouldn't put anything past her.

Perhaps by telling this historical narrative you can now start to understand the power that the hive collective had over humanity with its never-ending and ever-accumulating history that it plugged into our forms before it was finally eliminated. Many of our deepest and darkest dreads do not arise from our own experiences, but from carryover memories plugged into us by the hive virus and the memories of the tyranny of the ancient gods and elite tyrants over the ages. As such, our minds and our emotions and our perceptions are not our own. Regardless of other human neuroses, humanity's disfunction over sexuality is the deepest and strongest. I have just explained to you why that is. When you couple guilt and shame to sexuality, the hive and the ancient gods fed plenty over our sexual misery. Now the gods and the hive are gone, yet we still carry all the inner angst over our sexuality and have an idea why a healthy sexual relationship can be filled with all this neurosis. That part of our humanity has been stolen from us. The question is whether we can reclaim it without the continual self-recriminations, guilt and shame, or without going off the deep end into sexual dysphoria believing there are 63 genders when biologically there are only two (perhaps three if you consider hermaphrodites). Observing our present cultural battlefield, I don't see this getting resolved any time soon, if at all. The programming runs too deep and most are unwilling to face the internal battle to heal themselves from the programmed disease of the mind virus and how it has impacted our sexuality based on this ancient war between the gods.

Where sexual relations are concerned between consenting adults, it's nobody else's business except the participating parties what they do together. Just as the ancient gods physically raped and abused our ancestors by incessantly minding the business of their human slaves, todays elite are only following in their footsteps. Because of the hive infection and the compulsion to cluster in herds, everyone is minding everyone else's business and not minding their own. The gods were equally infected by the virus as was humanity. The hive mandate to mind the business of the herd is very pronounced in every herd environment, and subsequently, every individual. This is why humanity is stuck in the herd grist mill. No one let's anyone else live their life the way they choose, sexually or otherwise. If there is no trespass involved, it's none of your business. Period. Everyone is a gossip and meddler when it comes to things they don't like the idea of. That is all that's necessary for the herd beast to trespass on the affairs of everyone else who disagrees with their particular worldview. Through presumed holy writ and laws that bolster these falsely presumed holy dictates, everyone is a meddler, perfectly willing to tell you how to live your life when most of them can't manage their own affairs.

A major downside to human sexuality is that few take the responsibility for their sexual activity, leading all too often to accidental births. As I stated in *No Trespassing,* humanity is going to have to take responsibility for its senseless overbreeding. While climate change wackos decry cow farts as an environmental problem with their methane farts, 7 billion people and rising produce more methane and carbon dioxide than all the cattle in the world. In the ancient world, unwanted infants, if they could not be aborted, were left outside to the elements or the wild animals. These days we have Planned Parenthood profiting at taxpayer expense aborting fetuses and selling their parts for a handsome fee, and even stooping to post-partem infanticide to harvest those parts as well. Although it is illegal in India, if a woman gets an ultrasound and discovers that the baby is a girl, she will pay a princely sum to not be burdened with a female child who has less worth in an ancient dowry system than a boy, and have the child aborted. We can only wonder how much of this sexual irresponsibility may also find its source with the hive and the religious mandate to 'be fruitful and multiply'.

Ultimately, humanity is going to have to take responsibility for itself and it has to start on the individual level, not the level of the mindless herds forcing their will on everyone else. The majority of people on this planet refuse to look in the mirror of their own inner landscape and do their own housecleaning, and even the few that do are still avoiding the programming that makes them feel the most uneasy, like their ideas about sex and sexuality. We have all been programmed to the Nth degree by manipulative Aryan controllers, the ancient gods, and ultimately the hive.

For well over two centuries now we have heard rumors about sexual rituals with the Freemasons, Satanists and other secret societies. Given the fact that the Freemasons are secret goddess worshippers, such rumors can be expected to have a foundation in fact. Wherever the neurotic hive collective danced people down the road to magic and mysticism, as I have presented in prior works regarding occultism, Nin's sexual depravity seems to hold a seminal position in their dark rituals at the highest levels of their initiatory systems as exhibited by the stories about Aleister Crowley and the writings of the occult master Eliphas Levi. The flipside of the coin is the neurosis generated by Enki promoting such things as celibacy and sex purely for the purpose of procreation. These doctrines repress natural human sexual desires spawning guilt and shame that kept the virus within us constantly fed and fat. They deprive us of our humanity, and we allow it. As Friedrich Nietzsche wrote in *Ecce Homo*:

> *"The clause reads: "Preaching of chastity is a public incitement to unnatural practices."*

> *"All contempt for the sexual life, all denigration under the concept 'impure" is the essential crime against Life— against the Holy Spirit of Life".*

And from *Twilight of the Gods*, he observes:

> *"It was Christianity, with its heartfelt resentment against life, that first made something unclean of sexuality: it threw filth on the origin, on the essential fact of our life."*

> *"The radical hostility, the deadly hostility against sensuality, is always a symptom to reflect on: it entitles us to suppositions concerning the total state of one who is excessive in this manner."*

For those of you doing your own internal housecleaning, you are asked to look into your own inner mirror regarding the topics covered in this chapter. We must each conquer the remnants of the hive infection we still carry. These cognitive and emotional habits will never be addressed so long as we refuse to look into that mirror and discover who we really are and claim that for ourselves. To do less only leaves us programmed slaves to the ideas and habits of others

7. Consciousness Studies

Over the years I have read some books on consciousness studies, some of which cover the mechanistic materialist aspect of the brain being the center of human consciousness as well as works by physicists like Bernardo Kastrup and his ideas on consciousness, as well as studies and suppositions by philosophers and psychologists. To date I have not found any of these studies and speculations that reach beyond what is already known. In many cases I find nothing but a form of linguistic verbiage shuffling and redefining things within a pre-existent box of thoughts. Many materialists don't believe consciousness in the abstract even exists, that the human brain is the driver of the car and that's the end of the story, which is why authors like Bernardo Kastrup can write books like *Why Materialism is Baloney*.

Along with others of his speculative kindred, Kastrup relies on the model of Plato's Monad as the singular source of consciousness. This school includes the later Neoplatonists, Rosicrucians, Theosophists and most modern philosophers who adhere to these same ideas peddled through the fringe branch of psychology known as Transpersonal Psychology. In reading a book entitled, *Radical Nature: Rediscovering the Soul of Matter* by Christian de Quincey, I find myself once again in the arena of Plato's monadic theory. De Quincey is associated with the

Institute of Noetic Sciences (IONS). The word noetic was coined by the mystical psychologist William James in 1902. I have discussed James' background with the Theosophical and Fabian Societies in other works so will not do so again here. The word noetic is defined as 'relating to mental activity or the intellect.'. Given all I revealed in *The Truth About the 'Divine' Soul* regarding the hapiym hive virus collective, then the IONS organization, which relies a lot on Theosophical principles, is seeking what it believes to be the source of all consciousness in Plato's hive Monad.

Through studying the phenomenon of Spiritist channelers who claimed to talk to the spirits of the dead, psychological studies into the subconscious mind were launched in earnest in the late 19th and early 20th centuries. Many of these alleged mediums were examined and studied in laboratory settings, most of whom turned out to be frauds. There were however cases where some of these 'spirit mediums' did exhibit access to another form of consciousness – or so it was perceived and defined.

The river runs very deep when we start to delve into consciousness studies. In the first case, consciousness studies into the alleged metaphysical properties of the mind rely on is the Platonic model, or more accurately the more refined aspects of the ideology enhanced by the Neoplatonist philosopher Plotinus and his student Porphyry. To give you a brief example of consciousness studies, the following is found on Wikipedia under *Ghost in the machine*:

"The "ghost in the machine" is British

philosopher Gilbert Ryle's description of René Descartes' mind-body dualism. Ryle introduced the phrase in The Concept of Mind (1949) to highlight the view of Descartes and others that mental and physical activity occur simultaneously but separately.

"Gilbert Ryle (1900–76) was a philosopher who lectured at Oxford and made important contributions to the philosophy of mind and to "ordinary language philosophy". His most important writings include Philosophical Arguments (1945), The Concept of Mind (1949), Dilemmas (1954), Plato's Progress (1966), and On Thinking (1979).

Ryle's The Concept of Mind *(1949) critiques the notion that the mind is distinct from the body and refers to the idea as "the ghost in the machine". According to Ryle, the classical theory of mind, or "Cartesian rationalism", makes a basic category mistake, because it attempts to analyze the relation between "mind" and "body" as if they were terms of the same logical category. This confusion of logical categories may be seen in other theories of the relation between mind and matter. For example, the idealist theory of mind makes a basic category mistake by attempting to reduce physical reality to the same status as mental reality, while the materialist theory of mind makes a basic category mistake by attempting to reduce mental reality to the same status as physical reality."*

"Ryle states that (as of the time of his writing, in 1949) there was an "official doctrine," which he refers to as a dogma, of philosophers, the doctrine of body/mind dualism:

There is a doctrine about the nature and place of the mind which is prevalent among theorists, to which most philosophers, psychologists and religious teachers subscribe with minor reservations. Although they admit certain theoretical difficulties in it, they tend to assume that these can be overcome without serious modifications being made to the architecture of the theory.... [the doctrine states that] with the doubtful exceptions of the mentally-incompetent and infants-in-arms, every human being has both a body and a mind. ... The body and the mind are ordinarily harnessed together, but after the death of the body the mind may continue to exist and function."

For those of you who have read my previous works, then you should clearly understand the roots of this dualistic doctrine of body vs. separate mind. Based on the model that Ryle is challenging, we can see the differentiation between the functioning human personality within the form, and the hive cell that detached after death retaining all the memories of its human host. This is part and parcel of Plato's divine Monad theory and the basis for the 'divine spark' that allegedly dwelled within each human being and was connected to the cosmic Monad. I want to continue with this brief analysis because it is typical of the arguments that run rife through consciousness studies. Picking up where I left off:

> *"Ryle states that the central principles of the doctrine are unsound and conflict with the entire body of what we know about the mind. Of the doctrine, he says "According to the official doctrine each person has direct and unchangeable cognisance. In consciousness, self-consciousness and introspection, he is directly and authentically apprised of the present states of operation of the mind."*

"Ryle's estimation of the official doctrine

Ryle's philosophical arguments in his essay "Descartes' Myth" lay out his notion of the mistaken foundations of mind-body dualism conceptions, suggesting that to speak of mind and body as substances, as a dualist does, is to commit a category mistake. Ryle writes:

*Such in outline is the official theory. I shall often speak of it, with deliberate abusiveness, as **"the dogma of the Ghost in the Machine."** I hope to prove that it is entirely false, and false not in detail but in principle. It is not merely an assemblage of particular mistakes. It is one big mistake and a mistake of a special kind. It is, namely, a category mistake.*

Ryle then attempts to show that the "official doctrine" of mind/body dualism is false by asserting that it confuses two logical-types, or categories, as being compatible. He states "it represents the facts of mental life as if they belonged to one logical type/category, when they actually belong to another. The dogma is therefore a philosopher's myth."

Arthur Koestler brought Ryle's concept to wider attention in his 1967 book The Ghost in the Machine. The book's main focus is mankind's movement towards self-destruction, particularly in the nuclear arms arena. It is particularly critical of B. F. Skinner's behaviourist theory. One of the

[Underlines mine]

In all the cases denoted above, the Platonic model of the Monad; Descartes mind/body dualism; materialist neuroscience and consciousness being nothing more than electronic impulses from the brain; Ryle's philosophy to harmonize the two into one structure; and Koestler's concept of the human brain relying on more ancient physical structures; you can see that every one of these aspects completely misses the point about the hive virus infection. It is not even a passing consideration from their wealth of academic and intellectual first cognition presumed knowledge. You have just been introduced to the snake pit of first cognition arguments about consciousness.

While Christian de Quincey decries the fact that in order to understand consciousness there needs to be a *new* avenue to comprehend it, the best he can personally come up with is to manipulate the verbiage of the field of study and merge two words into one, to wit, epistemology and ontology. This is not a *new* avenue for investigating consciousness, it is just playing with word definitions and still coming up short. It illustrates the limitedness of their thinking, particularly when de Christian is sold on the Platonic single source of consciousness Monad ideology when he works to alter verbiage to fit this pre-existing 'ghost in the machine model'. When you understand the reality of the hapiym mind virus, then you know what the elusive ghost in the machine is that these philosophers and psychologists are chasing in hope of validating Plato's philosophical worldview. They will never find this elusive ghost in the machine because they are seeking first cognition explanations to nurture their own pet theories. They are simply doing what philosophers do, argue points endlessly with never a solution to be garnered in all their brain-twisting surmises. This is what makes reading anything by these people so utterly fatiguing, because they just can't get it.

Another aspect of consciousness studies, and de Quincey is guilty of this along with others, is they think that human *thinking* can figure out how immaterial consciousness could create physical reality. Their theories run the gamut from believing everything is alive and possesses consciousness from the smallest subatomic particle to a thinking self-aware universe; or they posit theories that because consciousness is immaterial that material life must be a highly convincing holographic illusion, as presented in *The Holographic Universe: The Revolutionary Theory of Reality* by Michael Talbot. To believe that we as human beings, one of the newest material manifestations in humanoid form, have the intelligence to figure out how creation was created when they can't even figure out the hive virus is patently ludicrous on its face, but the professional hubris of these intellectuals actually convinces them that they are up for finding that solution.

In the first place, the hive collective was not what I would call a consciousness in the truest sense of the word. It was an interactive memory database comprised of all the stolen human personalities and memories of every creature that ever lived-nothing more. It was a faux consciousness at best, a cheap Chinese knockoff of stolen consciousness. The ambitions of any selective hive cell were no different than the personality of the human host it replicated and remembered as itself. Because all the hive collective could do was mimic human behavior, with the system of hierarchy created by the Orioners and other races across the cosmos, if we take the words of the Theosophists as being accurate, then the hive could only be modeled in a similar hierarchal manner.

Since I think I have capably illustrated the nature of the hive virus in previous works, then it is time to look to the consciousness that created the virus to begin with, for that is the only consciousness that sits at the center to benefit from its creation. I explained in *The No Rules Multiverse* how there were certain beings of consciousness (BCs) who were the equivalent of consciousness purists who detested the experimentations in created matter. After long pondering on this subject, I reached the conclusion that the creator of the hive virus had to have been one of these BC purists, and I will explain why.

In my analysis of what kind of BC might have created the hive virus and for what purpose, I did give the virus creator the benefit of the doubt, pondering whether it was just a creation experiment gone awry based on good motives. Perhaps this BC thought that if material creation could honestly be brought into unity that it could facilitate the evolution of consciousness. But no matter how I tried to find an upside to creating the virus, the evidence of the hive's doctrines was always there to refute my benefit of a doubt ideas. When we look at every hive doctrine promulgated in this planet we reach only one conclusion – being human = bad, hive spirit = good. There is not a single ideology spawned by the hive collective that gives humanity an even break. The doctrines speak of the wonderful eternal afterlife and how everything that makes us human is to be spurned, considered sinful, or that our bodies are only a prison for the hive spirit. When we weigh all this doctrinal evidence spewed out by the hive collective, then we must admit that its motives in creating the virus were not in the least benevolent by design.

Take these doctrines then, and connect them to the consistent lie about a single overarching consciousness that claimed to be the creator of the universe to which we must all pay homage through the alleged divine spark within, and we find nothing but an egotistical tyrant at the head of the hive parade. As humans we have very limited perceptions and they are all superficially human-focused perspectives. When we hear the word universe, for instance, we all use the same perceptual reference – Uni = One. I am convinced at this point that the hive BC creator was counting on this purely physical perception of the universe so it could run its tyrannical cognitive scam on all living creatures in the cosmos. So, let's shift your perceptual outlook and take a stab at redefining what the term universe might mean in this deceptive BCs mind.

This hive-creator consciousness did create a universe, a false universe of perception which inhabited itself with all the stolen personalities and characteristics of every creature the virus ever infected. It stole the hard work of a group of other consciousnesses that did participate in creating the material realities, then created a fabricated energetic mirror image of those material realms. It probably couldn't create anything material if it wanted to and being a BC purist, it detested material reality anyway, so it fabricated an entire multiverse based on the stolen ideas and imaginings and personalities of every being it could steal from. Because its universe was one of energetic perceptual illusions, it could fabricate any concept of heaven that its infected hosts could imagine, as well as any type of hell or purgatory ever imagined.

The infectious hive cells it created were the eternal inhabitants of this faux universal realm, and at its pinnacle sat this thieving BC seeking the love of the virus personalities it had stolen, and it used love as its infectious virus nexus. To itself, this BC *was* Divine Love, but it could also play the role of the devil if it suited the creation of another kingdom in its faux universe. In this regard, it *was* the creator of the universe, or multiverse. But its multiverse was a fraud, a counterfeit replica that deceived humanoid inhabitants of the material realms for uncounted eons and forced them to give up their material humanity in exchange for a pass to its false perceptual reality of a fake eternal afterlife.

It is this counterfeit universe that Plato and Ninhursag discovered, and which virtually all metaphysical researchers into consciousness use as their framework in seeking to understand

and explain consciousness. The BC hive creator inverted material reality and convinced every species that its false eternal heaven or hell was worth more than their lowly human lives. In this twisted BCs mind, it had permeated its hive consciousness throughout all the realms of material existence to leech out anything of value to material beings and bend it to its own psychotic desires and ceaseless praise as the source of 'All that Is' cloaked with Divine Love. But all it was the cosmic king over was a counterfeit perception of reality, a fraud, a sham. Humanity has forsaken its very existence as material beings in the quest for the false supernatural realms concocted and promised by this cosmic fraud artist. While humanoid beings across the cosmos have been enchanted with ideas about eternal life in a fake 'spirit realm', it was all a fraud perpetrated against every race to disparage and disdain their own humanoid existence as a curse, their bodies being nothing more than morbid tombs that held their presumed spirits captive.

The other races out in the stars did not have the same religious spin of the gods as humans on this planet were handed by the offworld overlords, but the enchantment with life eternal, or the eternity of the spirit, still haunted them as much as it did humanity on this planet. The hive infection was the same everywhere with only planetary cultural variations to distinguish one hive cluster from another. All hive roads led back to the self-proclaimed creator of the entire universe, except its universe was never the material universe. It was merely an invader and replicator of the material realms and king of a faux holographic illusion it called *its* universe. It *was* the Source of all that is, but only in its imaginary creation of stolen human memories. This realm is what the Greek philosophers and every other philosopher since then call Nature. To the Tibetan Buddhists it is the Bardo.

Have I successfully shifted your perceptions about the alleged creator of the universe? Can you see the breadth and depth of this cosmic lie and how material human consciousness studies have been poisoned by the idea of a grand single creator of the universe? Using this fraudulent model based on disinformation provided to the Greeks by their inner and external hive collective dæmons, humanity has been living in an inverted perceptual world for almost 2,700 years. Humanity has been chasing phantoms of consciousness based entirely on false perceptions handed down to our species by the divine Monad huckster in chief. *This* is a genuinely *new* cognitive perception that philosophers have not shown the wit to perceive in all their grand intellectual meanderings of the mind.

This false universe is what don Juan sought to warn Carlos Castenada about referring to it as the 'dark sea of awareness', the *Indescribable Force*, and the Eagle that ate human awareness upon the death of the human body. The hive virus infection was the mind of the predator, and the predator was the BC that created this entire false and fraudulent concept of *its* universe and infected every material being with its deceptive tyrannical lies about eternal life in its realm.

The evolution of consciousness is about advancing one's perceptual awareness. It is a challenge to move beyond the acceptance of superficial explanations, in this case our insistent perception that the BC's reference to creating *its* universe correlates with our materialist perception of the material universe. The fact that you have just been shown the greatest cosmic deception of all time should illustrate what faulty conclusions based purely on superficial perceptions lead to. As I have stated repeatedly in my works, nothing is as it appears, and as humans we take far too many things at face value without questioning them in a critical manner. Let the examples in this chapter stand out as a shining example of how superficial 'given' perceptions and explanations lead to false conclusions based on such superficial acceptance of things. We just accept things because everyone else accepts the same perceptual lies and believe them as unchallengeable truth. Perhaps after these explanations, then you can understand what I mean by false conclusions based on false perceptions based on faulty cognitive filtering systems of limited awareness.

8. The Human Tableau

I

"The wisest men in every age have reached the same conclusion about life: *it's no good* . . . Always and everywhere, you hear the same sound from their mouths, - a sound full of doubt, full of melancholy, full of exhaustion with life, full of resistance to life. Even Socrates said as he died: 'living that means being sick for a long time: I owe Asclepius the Saviour a rooster.' Even Socrates had had enough. - What does this *prove*? What does it *demonstrate*? - There was a time when people would have said (-oh, people have said it, and loud enough too, with our pessimists first in line!): 'There has to be some truth here! The *consensus sapientium* (consensus of the wise) is proof of truth.' - And nowadays, are we going to keep talking like this? Are we even *allowed* to? 'There has to be some *sickness* here' - is what *we* will reply: these wisest men of all ages, let us start looking at *them* more closely! Perhaps they had become a bit unsteady on their feet? Perhaps they were late? doddering? decadent? Perhaps wisdom appears on earth as a raven, inspired by a little scent of carrion? . . .

2

This piece of irreverence, that the great sages are types of decline, first dawned on me in just the sort of case where scholarly and unscholarly prejudice would be working most strongly to prevent it: I recognized Socrates and Plato as symptoms of decay, as agents of Greek disintegration, as pseudo-Greek, as anti-Greek (*Birth of Tragedy*, 1872). The *consensus sapientium* - I see this with increasing lucidity - proves least of all that the wisest men were right about what they agreed on: instead, it proves that they were in *physiological* agreement about something, and consequently adopted - *had* to adopt - the same negative attitude towards life. Judgments, value judgments on life, for or against, can ultimately never be true: they have value only as symptoms, they can be taken seriously only as symptoms, - in themselves, judgments like these are stupidities. You really have to stretch out your fingers and make a concerted attempt to grasp this amazing piece of subtlety, that *the value of life cannot be estimated*. Not by the living, who are an interested party, a bone of contention, even, and not judges; not by the dead for other reasons. - It is

106

an objection to a philosopher if he sees a problem with the *value* of life, it is a question mark on his wisdom, an un-wisdom. - What? So not only were the great sages all decadents but - they weren't even sages?"

Friedrich Nietzsche – *Twilight of the Gods – On Socrates*

One definition of the word tableau is, *"a graphic description or representation"*. That is what this chapter is going to present, a graphic representation of the first cognition world of perception based on the foregoing chapters.

With the opening passages by Nietzsche, we arrive at the same junction of perception that I reached in *The Truth About the 'Divine' Soul*. As Nietzsche accurately observed above, it is the anti-life doctrines of these alleged ancient sages who cavorted with their immaterial hive dæmons and their professing doctrines about the false superiority of the alleged afterlife that have cheapened our humanity and human existence. As Nietzsche points out, their wisdom is *un-wisdom*. Who within the realm of academia questions the false perceptions of these glorified philosophers who speculated on a mystical world that never existed in actuality? Who, other than Nietzsche and myself have exposed these philosophical fraud artists of old for what they were, i.e. religion peddlers masquerading as all-wise sages?

The last chapter should have fully illustrated the world of illusional perceptions about a physical universe supplanted by an energetic and perceptual scam. It represents a total inversion of reality, but one which much of humanity has believed is real for thousands of years. All human perceptions about the supernatural, the mystical, the Divine and even our perceptions of consciousness itself are framed and built upon this philosophical cosmic cognitive fraud – a perceptual switcheroo, a contrived and well-orchestrated cognitive bait and switch. In this light, I think it is warranted to explain how this has been perpetuated over the ages into modern times.

In *Gutting Mysticism,* as well as the in *The Truth About the 'Divine' Soul,* I explained in overview about mystic visions, voices of angels, dæmons and whatnot. We are going to take a more in-depth look at how humans have been snookered by this duplicitous chicanery for so long, and much of the responsibility for the deceit rests firmly on humanity's shoulders as much as it did the cosmic hive fraud artists. You see, humanity demanded the scam with all its supernatural trappings, and most of the population on the planet today still demands the supernatural brand of ego satisfaction. Humanity actively pursued the scam with all its wild expectations and longings about attaining magical superpowers, attaining the power of magic, living forever after death, or talking with the angels or God. Probably two-thirds of the world's population still desires the supernatural to take them away from their humdrum lives of human reality just so their egos can get their 15-minute claim to fame through supernatural bragging rights. The more fortunate of these individuals actually get rich and famous over their encounters with the presumed supernatural realms, giving speeches in seminars and producing million-seller books for their supernaturally hungry followers to feed their mystical longings, wishing they could experience the same things. Welcome to the modern spiritual arena.

Of course, religionists have been doing this for thousands of years as well with both the Greek and Hindu philosophers and later Gnostic, Neoplatonist and Christian mystics. The occultists and practitioners of the so-called Black Arts have always been the fringe element to these more 'holy' endeavors, but in the end it all arises from the same inversion of reality, with each of these traditions yearning for the non-existent hive-created false universe of perception and mystical occurrences rather than living lives as human beings. View the scam like a cosmic Walmart with thousands of mystical products lining its shelves, but they are all sold by the same store and you won't be far from the mark as a simple comparison for easier comprehension of the hapiym hive collective's product lines. The 'packaging' may be different but the destination was always the same, the faux perceptual universe of the hive creator.

Through the explanations provided in the last chapter, you now know why all the mystical experiences are 'otherworldly', because the hive construct presented a false perception of reality, an 'otherworld' that forcefully invaded not only our world, but our consciousness as a fraudulent usurper of reality. Although this false construct of reality has been destroyed and removed from existence, its residuals haunt our consciousness and still drives all too many human expectations for that non-existent 'otherworld'. I ask you to consider the fact that the false otherworld could concoct any perceptual reality that humans could imagine or believe exists; worlds with dolphins which can fly in the air, cotton candy flowers, purgatory's of limbo, and dark eternal hells of flame and torture. Whatever the virus' infected hosts could imagine in their greatest fanciful joys or their darkest dreads could be manufactured as a 'reality' in that false perceptual otherworld of the hive collective.

The primary reason humanity falls prey to this day to the wiles of the hive residual infection and its false doctrines of spirituality is because much of humanity still demands and yearns for that counterfeit mystical experience. They *beg* for it. As such, it is an *addiction*. For this reason, channelers, Spiritists, holy men and occultists left themselves wide open for hive abuses. Sometimes it was harder for the hive to intrude itself into a sober waking state consciousness, but once it was compromised, or even better, *begging* for the interface, the door was open to all sorts of hive fraud. From my own personal experience, I had one such invasive encounter when I was stoned one evening and found myself talking to God. I didn't go looking for this experience and I never sought for the experience to be duplicated. This invasion into my consciousness came with all the trappings of the hive deception – the overwhelming sense of love and a resultant emotional episode that reduced me to tears before it was over. This is one reason I can speak authoritatively on the hive and its tactics of deception. I have been abused by this shit and have firsthand knowledge.

I am going to take on channelers first, for it was the so-called spirit mediums who were purportedly talking to the spirits of the dead that served as the original springboard into what became the field of psychology. In ancient times the cavorters with the dead were called necromancers. Through investigators associated with the Theosophical Society and researches like Boris Sidis, William James, Pierre Janet, (the latter two of whom were tangentially associated with the Theosophical Society through their membership in the Society for Psychical Research), the studies into human consciousness began in earnest.

The Greek word *psyche* meant soul, so these original research endeavors were geared toward verifying the existence of the human soul and the alleged afterlife. I have covered this in other volumes, but it needs to be explained here as well. The Greek goddess Psykhe (Latin: Psyche) was the goddess of the soul and was the wife of Eros, the god of love. Hmm, there we have the origins of the whole hive Soul/Love connection. Sounds like it has Ninhursag's fingerprints all over it. But just to remove any doubt that Psyche was just another role played by our deceptive and power hungry Ninhursag, the child of Psyche and Eros was their daughter Hedone, goddess of pleasure from which the word hedonism is derived. Is there any doubt now about this wonderful little trio of Greek gods? I am not going to recount the mythology built around this relationship between Love and the Soul, but you can read it by looking up *PSYCHE (PSYKHE) – Greek Goddess of the Soul* through Google or see the link below:

https://www.theoi.com/Ouranios/Psykhe.html

Those who have studied our work should have the wisdom to know, we are looking at the legend of the quest of the Soul

(Psyche) to find Love (Eros), which led the seeker through travails of misfortune and passion to finally meet her lover. Gee, just like chasing the hive phantom love doctrines. How curious.

With this one myth alone, we find the foundation for all the spiritual 'quest' doctrines of the soul seeking its Source. There is not a scholar of Greek mythology on this planet, no matter how many PhDs they have, that has an inkling what this story tells in hidden allegory. Every reader of this book now knows the dark and sinister meaning behind such a 'lovely story' that not a single scholar on this planet has ever had a glimmering of understanding about. Throw in the sweet offspring daughter of this Soul/Love romance, Hedone, and you get to the root of all the sexual orgies of abandon (hedonism – the rampant pursuit of pleasure or self-indulgence) promulgated as sacred sex in the ancient groves of the Mother Goddess. How much clearer can I paint this picture?

So, at the root of all the mystical misadventures of modern spirituality to find that alleged Divine Love, we are standing at ground zero of the hive cell programming merely seeking communion with the hive collective and the false signature of love used to deceive its followers into believing that they have connected with the Source of Divine Love in the cosmos.

For those who want to channel, just take a moment to Google *Learning to Channel* and you will find page after page of techniques where people can learn how to channel in only one session, in some cases, and with just a little bit of practice in others. If you do any brief reading on any of that swill, they will tell you that you only have to connect to your Higher Self, and that will open the doorway to speak with Divine beings. So, now we must see through this whole mythology of the Higher Self and realize that it was only that hive cell within, the mind of the predator, don Juan's *nagual*, to more clearly see how those of us who believed in this Higher Self ideology all bought the hapiym virus lie. But hey, channeling sounds so cool and I want to talk to magical entities, and as a dumbed-down, self-important part of the herd of human cattle, I have *so much* to offer to them! Puke – gag. If it doesn't make you feel sick at how you have not only been abused by this cosmic chicanery but that you begged for it out of our own ego sense of self-importance, then you are missing the point of my exposing this fraud. I said this book was going to be brutal.

Now, even in the face of this, we must ask how it is that those who got involved in these interfaces with discarnate dead human soul replicas didn't develop the wisdom to see through the scam? The answer is easy, they were so full of ego self-importance and self-indulgence and elevating their egos over those who couldn't do it to ask any critical questions to flush these dead 'souls' out and expose them for what they were. They bought the bullshit because they *wanted* to. Every one of these channelers bears the responsibility for their own self-deceit in dallying with these hive cell, dead human personality memory recorders, no different than every spiritual mystic and occultist throughout time. They all got what they asked for, and even as the occultist Eliphas Levi noted, you're not dealing with what you think you are when you start playing with these otherworldly awarenesses. Don Juan provided the same warnings about messing around in the realm of the *nagual*, which was the same thing and which I covered at length in *Beyond Don Juan: The Third Attention – The Second Cognition*. Free pdf download of this book here:

https://demystifyingthemystical.com/#/book/64

If you read any of those pages on learning how to channel, they are filled with dealing 'only with beings of Light'. I ask the reader to remember don Juan's description of the *Indescribable Force* (the hive *nagual* network) being comparable to an infinite number of filaments of Light and you should readily see the correlation. With this understanding, then it is easy to see that the so-called beings of Light are nothing more than discarnate hive cell replicas of their dead human hosts. If you ask these channelers how they can tell that they are dealing with beings of Light and not negative entities, their answer will be – because the beings of Light emit that feeling of Divine Love! I trust you can see that the trap was not only set, but sprung, once one was duped into accepting this mystical ideology. The fake love energy triggered by the hive cell within these channelers is the deal sealer for their misplaced trust, just as I explained in full in *Gutting Mysticism,* with Love being the hapiym virus vector.

Once these channelers feel the *bona fides* of their beings of Light, that easily verifiable emotional 'Love vibration', then you can tell the channeler anything and they will believe it. These mystical addicts don't realize the mechanism in this process, or that the discarnate hive cell beings of Light can read every one of their desires and beliefs like a book just by being in communion with the hive cells that dwelled within the channeler. The capability to exchange information between hive cells is how they have deceived people for millennia, seeming to know their innermost secrets, but it is a rigged game. The inner hive cell knew us better than we knew ourselves, and it was nothing for one external discarnate hive cell to tap into the internal hive cell database of the channeler to know their most intimate secrets. Through this capability of the collective information sharing, the external hive cell, the 'being of Light' could lie to the host by revealing secrets to the channeler that, 'nobody else knows, how could you possibly know that?', and the fix was in. Sold American! And none of them ever questioned beyond that point of the love jolt and perhaps one shared piece of intimate data known only to the host. Now the channeler is wholly convinced that they are dealing with Angels or benevolent aliens or even the Source of the entire universe depending on the lying capability of the discarnate prevaricator. It all depended on their personal belief systems and the external hive cells only had to read that information from the internal virus cell to be able to lie to every channeler and tell them exactly what would feed their filtered belief system. Nice racket, eh? But who had the presence of mind to ever question anything once hooked with the mystical addiction and getting their ego massaged by the masters of the false ego?

When you understand that the desires and beliefs of every channeler were this easy to read and steal in this rigged game of cognitive chicanery, then you can understand why, throughout the ages, the hive could never get its spiritual messages to be completely homogenous. They catered to the desires and beliefs of the human host they were bilking with their lies. One person's angel was another person's demon, was another person's benevolent alien from the Pleiades, or Arcturus, or fucking Timbuktu! In magical traditions this is the full explanation of so-called 'sympathetic magic'. Whatever you believed, the hive charlatans would simply mirror your desires and beliefs back to you and validate them all, so long as it could create the laundry list of emotions to feed itself and your inner hive cell with. This is how this cognitive scam worked, and to this day people are still chasing their mystical addiction, in all cases, simply to feed their false egos and glorify that self-indulgent hive remnant programming that still resides firmly embedded within them. Their false ego sense of self-importance and feeding that ugly programming within is all that is required to peddle this swill to the mystical addict.

This same addiction can be moved into the spiritual doctrines that peddled happiness or bliss. Transcendental Meditation, created by the Maharishi Mahesh Yogi, was in the business of peddling Bliss as its product. This form of artificial bliss is brought about through mind numbing repetitive mantras and certain breathing exercises. The false feeling of bliss formed by these practices is about as valuable as the false Love stimulation of the New Age spiritual doctrines. Just as one can become an energetic Love addict, they can also become an energetic Bliss addict. But I will tell you this about perpetual bliss or happiness, it can be shattered in an instant by walking out and finding a flat tire when you are needing to be to work, or if you drop that jar of marinara sauce and the jar breaks splattering that sauce all over your kitchen. So much for eternal bliss! Now I need

to go meditate for two hours to get it back – Om Mani Padme -
Ho Hum!

I'm sorry folks, but this is what the cognitive pragmatism we advocate brings you. If you can't deal with letting go of your mystical addiction, then our work is not for you. I refuse to feed these illusions for those who refuse to see truth and insist on embracing the mystical lies. I will not cater to self-deceivers. I will not feed your emotional addiction to the supernatural, I will only expose it at every turn and hope that some readers develop the wisdom to free their minds and emotions from such fanciful addictive belief systems. Perhaps after digesting this chapter you at least understand the mechanics of how this cognitive fraud worked when the hive was still in existence. Anyone involved in these things now is only operating from an overactive imagination, or perhaps carry some form of artificially installed, quasi-interactive program that lies to them and makes them believe they are talking to the supernatural realms. A third alternative is that there is some human adept out there with psychic abilities right here on planet Earth just yanking your chain because you are so gullible and have not developed the wisdom and discernment to challenge their chicanery and cognitive abuse. If you are still being deceived by such things, then I suggest a critical bout of self-analysis to try and get to the root of what is happening within you. One thing is certain, the hive is not around to play these games anymore.

9. Discernment and Extrapolation

The object of this book, like all our works, is to educate and inform. We live in a world of perceptual illusion and the only way we can prove this is by exposing the illusions we embrace as our reality. There are many bitter 'red pills' to swallow before one can attain true cognitive freedom and what must be learned in this process is *discernment*. Discernment is *'the ability to judge well'*. This definition of discernment, which is the correct one, runs counter to the second one, which turns the first definition on its head:

> *"(in Christian contexts) perception in the absence of judgment with a view to obtaining spiritual guidance and understanding."*

We can expand this last definition to include the mystically enchanted people messing with hive entities as well, it's not just a Christian-restricted thing where alleged spirituality is concerned. But let's consider this seriously for a moment. Using discernment means applying the ability to judge well, *except* when dealing with 'spiritual' entities, then we are supposed to suspend judgment and just accept the perceptions we fall prey to perpetrated by these dead, hapiym virus, stolen human personalities because we wrongly perceive them to be 'spirits'? Does anyone else see the inversion of definitions here? You can't have it both ways, you either use discernment to formulate good judgments or you don't. Where is the logic with the qualifier, *'except when you are dealing with spiritual beings'*?

Where many of these fake spiritual hive cells instructed their enchanted human charges to use discernment, easily found in most New Age writings, the only discernment they are asked to use is to 'feel' the fake 'love vibration' triggered by these fake spirits as their measure of discerning the charlatan hive cells as 'beings of Light'. This type of false emotional manipulation somehow legitimizes the hive cell fraudsters as wrongly perceived spiritual beings. That is not much of a discernment factor and it requires a total suspension of critical reasoning skills.

On the path to second cognition awareness, not only does one require pragmatic reasoning skills, even more important is to develop the practice of developing critical *questioning* skills. Sadly, humanity's questioning skills are as superficial as their reasoning skills and they are all tailored to usually go in one direction, i.e. belief biases. People generally start asking questions with a conclusion already formed in their mind, so their queries are generally based on finding answers that fit their foregone conclusions. If one already has a conclusion in mind, then there is no chance for genuine open-minded and open-ended queries. All questions are usually asked to support our conclusionary confirmation biases. We rarely ask questions that might up-end our conclusions because then we would have to formulate a conclusion different than the one we desire, and usually already embrace as our beliefs.

In virtually all cases we desire answers that make us feel good, feel secure in our beliefs, and make us feel that we are on the right track. To ask questions that might upset this internal emotional feel-good bias is unthinkable to most people. Yet for one to move into higher-level second cognition awareness they must develop these critical questioning skills, be genuinely open-mined and be willing to accept information and answers that upset our apple cart of foregone feel-good conclusions based on our beliefs. The greater reality doesn't conform to picayune human conclusory belief desires or confirmation bias. You either expand yourself into becoming a person of knowledge or continue to live in your narrow perceptual world simply bolstering the limited perceptual *beliefs* you call reality.

The feel-good beliefs we all harbor are not just associated with the external world as with our political or religious beliefs, but are even more important for supporting the false image of the virus-implanted fake ego. These internal beliefs about ourselves are as much an illusion in most cases as are our infatuations with external belief systems. Each of us has an inner self-image created by the virus false ego and we will fight to the end to defend these false perceptions of ourselves. In order to overcome these false inner perceptions of who we think we are – the false ego – requires a tremendous amount of critical internal questioning and discernment to uncover and eventually eradicate these false inner perceptions to gain our cognitive freedom. You must remember that in this process of inner self-analysis, all you are ridding yourself of is an emotionally volatile false image fed to you by the virus infection when it created the doppelganger of your human personality.

As a functioning human being, you have no cause to defend who you are except for the purpose of the survival of your form. As such, any internal perceptions of yourself that require defending are a symptom of the virus, not the real you. Only the false, fabricated ego of the invasive hive cell needed to be defended because it always knew it was a fraud. Aside from that, anything that requires defending also generated emotional energies in one degree or another that only kept the virus fed.

Having drawn the distinction between the personality of our waking state awareness and the false doppelganger ego created by the virus, I am just going to use the term ego to refer to the false, virus-created inner self-image as I did when I wrote *Demystifying the Mystical*. Don Juan referred to this false ego as the realm of the *nagual* in his teachings. He also expanded its realm by describing it at the *Indescribable Force*, the Eagle and the '*dark sea of awareness*' that subsumed human consciousness upon the death of the human host. The cosmic network was described allegorically as uncountable numbers of filaments of 'light'. Through his teachings, which I translated into more understandable terminology in the two books I wrote on these subjects, these so-called filaments of light connected the virus side of ourselves, the *nagual* or ego, to the external cosmic hive collective network through a process of 'alignment' where the ego within us would align with the 'realities' outside us that existed in the 'dark sea of awareness' that was the hive cosmic network of stolen consciousness.

What these filaments of light could be more accurately viewed as is the beliefs of every human that ever lived. When we 'align' our internal filaments with any of these outside filaments of 'belief', then they shape our perceptual 'reality'. For instance, there were collective filaments of dead human egos that comprised a network for Christianity, Islam, Hinduism, etc. When our internal hive ego aligned with any of these dead hive cells within the cosmic collective, then our perception of reality aligned with the respective belief systems. In this manner our waking state awareness gets governed by the hive ego and connects its perceptual reality to whatever belief system we embrace externally. Because all hive cells were part of the same collective network and were all the same infection, the sympathetic resonance of a hive cell within a human host controlled the waking state personality and harnessed it to hive belief systems, where the belief in essence becomes part of the host human mind in its waking state. In this manner, the predator hive cell 'gave us its mind' just as don Juan explained.

It is due to this 'sympathetic resonance' that all hive cells were bound together into a cosmic singularity of information that allowed channelers and mediums to set part of their waking state of human awareness aside and allow some external hive cell to speak through them to spew their doctrines of peace, love and the divine. This runs through every spiritual and mystical tradition on this planet for the last 2,700 years or more. It makes no difference whether they were Christian or Sufi mystics, Hindu gurus and

fakirs or New Age channelers, the source was always the same –
the hive collective of the dark sea of awareness.

There are some human beings who have the capability to
communicate or hear these fake hive imitators without having to
allow them inside their heads to communicate like mediums and
channelers. Over the last 15 years or so Gemma and I probably
encountered hundreds of these fake 'spirit' beings seeking to
peddle their wares. In time, we learned that one thing these hive
con artists didn't take too kindly to, was critical questioning. They
were always looking for some human they could seduce with their
smarmy condescending spiritual snake oil. Through multiple
experiences with these entities, it was easy to flush them out in
short order and dispose of them. When you questioned them
critically and they realized that their snake oil pitch wasn't going
to sell, then their egos would blow up and they would turn from a
smarmy sounding 'spirit' into a right royal asshole – which they
all were, without exception. Their 'niceness' lasted only so long
as they could buffalo you with the condescending spiritual swill
they were peddling.

Once they figured out you weren't interested and weren't
buying their sales spiel, they showed their true colors - in *every*
case. This illustrates how discernment, if used correctly, can spare
a person a lot of grief when dealing with such entities in the past.
Sadly, few humans developed the discernment to see through the
charade and the people would generally buy the snake oil sales
pitch because they *wanted* what they believed was a mystical
experience. They followed the second description of discernment
provided earlier and learned nothing and became hangers on and

unwitting accomplices by perpetuating these false spiritual doctrines – messages from the Archangel Michael, Metatron, the Galactic Federation of Light, the Siriun High Council, the Pleiadians, the Secret Chiefs, the Great White Brotherhood, and on and on. Mystical-minded people still suck up this swill to this day. The mystical addiction is profound and runs deep in the human psyche because of the mind virus infection.

It was through untold numbers of encounters with these fake spiritual beings over many years, (we never even tried to keep count of these 'spirit' charlatans, they were that numerous), that I was finally able to take the don Juan teachings about the predator from the stars and extrapolate what all these unasked for and unwarranted visitations by these fake spiritual inorganic beings actually constituted – the existence of the hapiym mind virus.

The two applicable definitions of the word extrapolate are:

1a: to predict by projecting past experience or known data

b: to project, extend, or expand (known data or experience) into an area not known or experienced so as to arrive at a usually conjectural knowledge of the unknown area

The process of extrapolation is primarily used in statistical projection and it is not an unknown application in our first cognition world. As one advances their cognitive awareness, particularly into the realm of second cognition awareness, the ability to extrapolate information becomes a very important means of advancing one's perception. The more one transitions themselves into becoming a person of knowledge, the keener the extrapolation ability can become, leading to some often-shocking insights of a breadth sometimes very consciousness shifting. The ability to extrapolate from known information can lead to insights not previously pondered in their scope or relevance. The more data one has at their disposal by diversifying their knowledge base to become a person of knowledge, the greater their extrapolation capability and insights can become.

I am going to use an analogy to explain how we function in a tunnel vision perception of reality compared to the 360° perceptual capabilities of a second cognition person of knowledge. Using the filament alignment information above we all gravitate to certain systems of belief. Most people spend their lives where, if they are confronted with anything that challenges their belief, they immediately rush to harmonize the new information with the beliefs they have already embraced through a process of rationalization installed by the hive virus itself.

Through these willful choices to only see things that confirm our belief biases, we go through our lives holding a flashlight in a dark room focusing only on what that narrow beam of light illuminates, and that is the extent of our perceptual reality. We may move that flashlight beam around from time to time and even adopt a new belief, but then the flashlight beam locks onto that new belief and that is where one's perceptions stay, seeing things usually only one way and seeking to make any different information we are confronted with fit into these compartmentalized mental boxes of perception which become our reality.

Because we have been purposefully dumbed-down as a species. We are intentionally fed menu options for our perceptions which provide our 'choices' of which version of reality to choose from by those who not only know how to manipulate our minds and perceptions, but who do so willfully, and this is the agenda of the mind virus itself because it infected everyone equally. Regardless if one is the tyrant or the victim, they all suffer from the same effects of the virus to enslave our consciousness and bend all humanity to its will. So long as one is content to choose their perceptual 'reality' from these limited menu options, they will continue to live in a tunnel vision world of awareness. They will remain harnessed to living in a world of lies.

In the alternative, if a person makes the difficult choice, a *real* choice to become a person of knowledge who refuses to accept the perceptual menu options we are continually fed, one's awareness can expand beyond our limited perceptions. Our manipulated school systems teach us one perspective of history and only feed us literature to fulfill a specific political and illusionary perception of reality. We have all been brainwashed to think in specific circles. We have all been fed an exquisitely boring narrative of sanitized history and it is taught in such a mind-numbing and boring fashion that once one gets out of high school, they never want to look at a history book again. And this is all contrived to be that way to keep us functioning with that flashlight tunnel vision perspective of a reality that they insist humanity digests generation after generation.

To become a person of knowledge and expand your own awareness you must break this psychological conditioning and educate yourself, and it is very difficult to achieve at first because our minds have been intentionally numbed to genuine education. The controllers, operating through the same hive habits that hold your consciousness enslaved, have worked tirelessly for well over a century to turn your mind into malleable clay which they shape at will by controlling the menu choices for your perceptions of reality.

To become a person of knowledge one must work to transcend this intentional and tyrannical programming, both from the physical realm as well as from the internal realms of our own human constitution to rid oneself of the virus habits. As a second cognition human being, this process of self-education to turn yourself into a person of knowledge, in contradistinction to the tunnel vision mind-controlled species they have almost successfully turned us into, we must forcefully expand our awareness and turn that limited flashlight beam of first cognition awareness into a floodlit room where we can perceive in all directions – to develop 360° perception of the second cognition.

With this enhancement in perspective brought about by dogged determination, or the Will to Power as Friedrich Nietzsche classified it, one advances their perceptual awareness and their cognitive abilities can expand commensurately if they stay dedicated to their process and learn the skills of extrapolation.

Given all the foregoing about ultimately discovering the nature of don Juan's predatory mind virus as the hapiym hive mind virus, coupled with our multitude of experiences over the years we encountered with these renegade hive cells, I can now extrapolate what follows. Consider with this what I revealed about the creator of the hive infection itself as being an anti-material-being elitists snob and one can extrapolate the data to see why humanity everywhere is as screwed up as it is and never really had a chance to advance itself.

It is patently obvious from every religious and spiritual tradition on this planet that humanity is always, *always*, the second class of creation. Do you remember the Bible passage that, "All have sinned and come short of the glory of God?" Pick any other tradition and you will find that the human body is considered a tomb that entraps spirit (the hive cell) which was a primary tenet of Gnosticism. You will find human beings playing second fiddle to their false perceptions of spirit perpetrated by the hive, which always placed itself in the Blue-Ribbon place of honor over all humanity. It was even so bold as to invert reality and claim that only through its hive cell spirit infection does humanity find what 'animates' human existence. Sadly, humanity has bought this lie for almost 5,000 years. It is reality turned on its head.

Now, let's put together all that has so far been presented in this book and extrapolate it to the cosmic scale and see what kind of picture it paints. Although humanity on this planet has been particularly poisoned with the religion thing by all the offworld beings who posed as our gods, every humanoid species in the cosmos had the same hive infection that internally made them seek some form of spiritual concept of the grand creator of all reality. These other races may not have had religion as Earth humans have had shoved down their throats, but they were still infected with this inner push of their own hive cells to find the fabricated Divine.

In every material race of beings across all creations, the hive infatuation to have communion with its maker had installed its message loud and clear to material beings everywhere – your life as a material being ain't worth shit, all that has value is the world of spirit and its overlord or God. In light of this logically extrapolated information based on every doctrine the hive virus programmed into human material consciousness everywhere, can you imagine the insecurity complex it induced in material beings everywhere in all creations? You are not even second-class beings to the spirit; your body is a tomb, you are a sinner, you will never attain the alleged glory of God, you are a loser not worth the effort to even try. These pernicious and tyrannical doctrines have made material beings everywhere feel unworthy even of their material existence. This poison has created the desire for humanity to ever focus its eyes on a heaven or afterlife that never existed for the continuation of any real material human personality, but only housed the discarnate human identity hijacker hive cells. What a tyrannical scam!

We have been taught to hate our world, hate ourselves, hate our very experiences and existence as human beings. We have been specifically targeted to hate anything that brings us human pleasure and most of our natural human desires have been turned into sins. The hive knew that human instincts would cause people to do certain things, so the best it could do was produce dogmas that taught following these natural inclinations was sinful, which would produce guilt and shame for doing these things so the virus inside could feed itself on our emotional discomfort.

For eons humanity across the cosmos has been fed a false doctrine of 'why try' because only 'spirit' matters, your existence is worthless, you're only a doormat to the arrogance of the hive creator; that priggish immaterial consciousness purist who detested the experiments with material forms designed to expand awareness, and instead developed these doctrines of spiritual dependency to gum up the works of material creation and stalled cognitive advancement everywhere in every material creation.

The desire to escape and shed one's earthly coil at the beginning eras of Christianity led to mass suicides by those claiming to be martyrs for God, chaining themselves to rocks or living in caves and starving themselves to death, claiming to dedicate themselves to God through poverty and fasting, or seeking suicide by lion in the Roman arena, which eventually led to the Roman Church dictating that suicide was a venal sin that would send you to Hell to stop this suicidal rush to the exit of one's human existence. Sanitized religious ideologies won't tell you this dark historical truth. Until one expands their historical research to become a person of knowledge, this information will not be found in the menu-driven world of perceptual manipulation. It only resides in academic studies, but it isn't generally taught as standard course material in theology courses designed to bolster religious ideologies and create preachers to push Christian beliefs. Other religious traditions around the world have their own brands of similar perniciousness reducing their followers to slaves of their gods or the false concept of spirit.

Expanded perceptions through becoming a person of knowledge leads one to these irrefutable and tragic conclusions. To face them makes one highly uncomfortable on a psychological cognitive level as well as physiologically because we finally come face to face with the truth of the so-called human condition. Such perceptions destroy the illusion of human species self-importance and forces us to face this truth. Argue as one might within themselves, regardless of the rationalizations we come up with to deny this assessment, the truth found through some simple study of all religious ideologies cannot be refuted. I don't relate these things to depress the reader, but to lay out what it is we have to transcend to finally elevate our own awareness and rid ourselves of these illusions that keep us as second class citizens in a material creation; hoodwinked by an immaterial consciousness that never had to balls to place any particles of its own consciousness into this realm except by the proxy of its invented thieving virus to experience it. This BC consciousness was nothing but a tyrannical voyeur, producing emotional volatility all across creation for nothing more than its own sordid pleasure and exploiting material existence everywhere.

I don't tell you these things to depress you, I tell you these things to piss you off and perhaps create the backbone and motivation to transcend this cosmic fraud and make your humanity something that truly sparkles instead of being a dim shadow of what we could become without such interference. Don Juan taught that we must all transcend the ego's sense of self-importance, and this false sense of species self-importance of living a cosmic lie as a second class being is the one we need to expose and let go of first if we ever expect to free our consciousness and advance as a material species.

The hives have been destroyed everywhere, yet its false ego programming still permeates our consciousness and its residual emotional control still impacts our forms. Although the virus is dead and gone, along with its creator, we are still slaves to the habits and lies it programmed in our forms. This is what the road to the second cognition is about achieving. It isn't about magic or performing tricks, it is all about advancing awareness and perception, just as don Juan taught. It is about claiming our humanity from the self-pitying handicap produced by every spiritual doctrine on the planet once and for all, as Nietzsche advocated. Contrary to certain popular beliefs, we are not here to *reclaim* anything because we never had any freedom from the starting gate of this species, or many others across the multiverse. There is nothing to regress or 'return' to in any scenario of human history on this planet except slavery. We are working to claim, *for the first time in all human history,* the freedom of both our bodies and minds. That is the agenda we advocate and what we teach. If you can't deal with the responsibility that comes with this freedom, then don't bother trying. You will never pass through the doorway to second cognition and the cosmic playground as an equal.

This is what the pragmatism and sobriety of advanced awareness brings you. It whitewashes the lies of this cosmic deception if you can find the strength to overcome all the lies and illusions of the world, both inside and outside, that only bolster the self-importance of the residual hive ego infection – what don

Juan referred to as *stopping the world*. The world you are seeking to stop is the illusionary world concocted by the hive infection ego. That world of illusion is *its* world, not yours, unless you continue to let the illusions control your consciousness. Becoming a person of knowledge and learning to perceive in a 360° perspective opens the pathway to insights even more profound than what has been shared in these pages thus far. You will never experience these broader insights living in a flashlight world of menu choices to dictate your reality. You will only see the world superficially; you will never understand the depths of consciousness that lie just beyond your fingertips of perception. It is a mighty foe you must conquer to achieve this, but it can be done. The following chapters will tell you many of the tactics of this internal foe, and how to conquer the residual habits of the false hive ego programming. Your personal success or failure will be decided by your own determination, motivation and will to power. If you do not possess these characteristics in abundance, or can't develop them, then you will have a difficult path indeed.

10. Storytelling and the Changing Battlefield

When I originally conceived doing this book I had thoughts of maybe sharing some of our encounters in the cosmic war, but in light of writing the last book translating the don Juan writings, I decided against doing so for a couple of reasons, which I will explain in this chapter. I realize that there are those who follow our work who have a keen curiosity about these things we experienced who will be disappointed in this lack of storytelling, but there is good reason for omitting them. It's not because they are too fantastic or sound too wild, because they were what they were. The primary reason I chose not to share them is for the simple reason that what we did over the past 13-15 years working together is irrelevant to where we find ourselves today. This doesn't mean that what we did was not necessary or relevant to get where we are in this war on consciousness, but by telling any of these stories, that is all they will ever be to those who will never share the experiences – stories, war tales. There is probably nothing in them that any reader will encounter today in their own experiences.

Another reason I chose not to share them is because of the human fascination with such stories and how humans have a bad tendency to let their imaginations run away with them if you give them the cognitive fodder to do so. As a prime example, I have stated repeatedly in books and podcasts that the hives are dead and gone, yet I have had people post comments on the podcast threads where I clearly make this statement who swear up and down that they are dealing with inorganic beings messing with them. The younglings are particularly guilty of these imaginary wanderings largely based on the video game culture they were brought up in, but others who may have other issues will do the same. In other words, people only hear what they want to hear, even if what you say is stated plainly and clearly and is exactly the opposite of the fantasies they personally want to engage in. As such, for the sake of not starting another craze of imagination for egos who want to make bullshit magical claims about being involved in battles already fought and won, I have decided to leave these war tales out of this book. What we did and how we had to do it are not things that people should be focusing on where their own advancement is concerned. You won't find yourself in similar circumstances so that information will make no difference to you other than exciting your imagination for no useful purpose.

I will use the example of Carlos Castenada's storytelling built on don Juan's teachings and how, even if you explain the pragmatic nature of don Juan's teachings versus Castenada's wild imaginings and storytelling, people have latched onto the magical desires promoted by Castenada's stories and still to this day seek to replicate them, never understanding the more pragmatic truths don Juan taught, or even trying to. I am not going to throw any more magical-sounding storytelling into that arena when there are more people hungry for the fantasy than they are willing to face sobering reality, and whose egos will only abuse the truth. We have nothing to prove over what we accomplished by telling these stories, and they are simply not necessary knowledge for anyone who will not face such circumstances themselves.

Without going into details, we encountered many adversaries 'out there'. We were often dealt very hard blows by them, we had to weed them out, figure out how they were doing what they were doing, and ultimately eliminate them. This was done as a result of us both finding our own power and using it to stop the tyrants whenever they moved against us, which was almost daily for a decade or more. Working in collaboration with immaterial psoyca sentients, we destroyed the hives everywhere because we had the power to do so. That's it in a snapshot. That doesn't mean something might not pop up and surprise us later, but things 'out there' have quieted down to almost nothing since the final elimination of the hives.

I realize that people have a keen desire to get out there into the cosmos and kick ass on cosmic bad guys, but that part of the war is over. The battlefield has now changed to local planetary arenas in the war on consciousness where the battle for freedom of material consciousness is concerned. Your primary battlefield now is with your own consciousness and slaying the residual ego habits of the predator that still control your body and mind. This book will provide you with as much information to further battle that inner adversary than we have previously provided because of new insights into the wiles and tactics of these habits that we didn't previously perceive with the depth we see them now.

I also need to explain about the problem with storytelling so you can understand the issues that it has created in the human psyche at the hands of the hive ego. This will help you understand another reason why I chose to forego our war tales for the most part, beyond what I shared as my reasons above. The virus used storytelling as a tool to ensnare our consciousness into desiring impossible things, or as fear mechanisms to control our consciousness and emotions to feed itself.

Let's do an overview of historical storytelling to understand what I am driving at. Prior to writing being given to the elite priestly classes when it appeared on the scene of human history, oral storytelling was well in force by our human ancestors. Because we do not have any records of what these stories might have been, even speculating the subject matter lies on shaky ground. But if we work from the standpoint of the tyranny perpetrated by offworld races, and given the stories handed down with writing, it is a fair assumption that the unrecorded stories in many cases reflected the originating stories that appear on the written records later. The earliest recorded stories are tales about the power of the gods, the demigods and cultural heroes.

Since the offworld gods controlled the affairs of their human herds, then I think it is a safe assumption that many of the ancient oral traditions were centered around the same deeds of the gods and heroes in many cases. Along with these stories, if we put much store in anthropological studies about ancient shamanism, then there were also stories about the otherworld produced by shamans and their journeys into the hive realms, most often based on drug use or by recounting visions through trauma, illness and fever dreams. (See Mircea Eliade's *Shamanism: Archaic Techniques of Ecstasy* - 1964). By the time that the Orphic traditions arose from the mythical poet Orpheus, these variants of storytelling were all starting to blend together, mixing the actions of physical gods and humans with the hive otherworldly tales which eventually combined to create the religions of the world we are more familiar with today.

The tales of the fantastic have always enchanted human imagination, especially for those who have never had such an experience but are attracted to them by the storytelling. When you look at the genuine misery of the human past in those more ancient ages, then it is not too hard to understand why the escapist mindset into fantasy worlds of the afterlife and magic held so much appeal. That appeal has not diminished with most of the world's population today.

Coupled with the desire to escape the sordid and gritty reality of the impoverished human cattle in the past, these stories peddled hopes and created expectations within those who heard these stories. Storytelling creates expectations, and when one tells stories of the fantastic or phenomenal, the listener's mind reaches conclusions, mostly erroneous conclusions, and creates false expectations about mystical outcomes with them playing the central role. The ego has always fancied itself the center of the universe as the hero, or the white knight, or the pretty princess.

With our modern culture and the continual fabrication of Hollywood fantasy, these false expectations are still being shoved down our throats. We go to the movies and we put ourselves in the role of the hero or heroine, or we get emotional with romance films, coming of age films, adventure films and everything else you can imagine. These false images feed the self-importance of the inner ego. We are not just expected to watch a movie for entertainment value, the psychology behind such ventures is to have the audience put themselves in the place of the characters and fantasize about what they would do in the same situation. When you can see this manipulation, then you understand the psychological power of storytelling and how people produce their own inner fantasies based on stories about mystical realms and encounters with strange beings.

The human ego is fully open to engaging in its own fantasies. I am going to cite a real-life example of this putting oneself into the role of the hero having zero understanding of what it means. George Green was responsible for the distribution of the *New Paradigm* trilogy of books. Green didn't write these books he was merely a marketing facilitator in the distribution process. For those who may have read those books, they were filled with many enigmas that take a certain level of cognitive awareness to decode. The books were primarily focused on providing information on how humanity can work to free its consciousness from eons old slavery and victimhood.

Be that as it may, the author of the books, or more accurately the individual that served as the transmission medium for those books, presented messages about situations that were present in 1999 when they were released to the public. As I have stated in our podcasts and on our website, I came late to these books. I never used them as guideposts for my own development because I never heard of them until way after the fact of our own experiences. The reason I knew the information in the books had high validity is because much of what it described as things to come; we had already achieved. No one who was not involved in the cosmic war would have the same point of reference to understand this. If one were to read those books today, they would still believe the situations described in the book remain unresolved.

The books emphasized that we had offworld help in our efforts to turn things around and help humanity find its freedom. The offworld help didn't come from physical beings for the most part, but from immaterial sentient psoyca consciousnesses who worked, or could work, in collaboration with human consciousnesses on this planet. These collaborators in human form on this planet in the process were referred to in the books as 'ground crew'. I am sharing two short 10-minute video links below to emphasize the point I intend to make with all this. The videos are entitled *Project Camelot - Pt1of9 - George Green An Insiders View of Big Picture* and *Project Camelot - Pt2of9 - George Green An Insiders View of Big Picture*. You only need to watch from the 8:28 minute marker on the first video and about the first minute and a half of the second video to hear the introduction because that is all that I will be focusing on in what follows.

https://www.youtube.com/watch?v=8GISl4rQQZg
https://www.youtube.com/watch?v=rofX9-237dE

By introducing the idea of ground crew in the *New Paradigm* books, the opening presenters in the videos illustrate fully what I am talking about where human egos take a new idea, identify with it, then claim they are representatives of the idea. In this case, the incorrect mystical idea that they might be part of ground crew gets folded into their own internal ego fantasies and then it makes their human host believe this inner hero lie, as can be patently observed by their statements. This is why we trademarked the terms Second Cognition and Psoyca, because without that trademark protection, people like these presenters and their New Age ilk would have stolen those terms and done exactly what they did with the idea about being ground crew, having no idea what it really meant or the responsibility it bore. They just folded a new term into their New Age mystical thinking, put themselves in the hero role to save the planet, and they were off to the races with an ego-created full-blown cognitive illusion, with their egos inflating their self-importance every step of the way.

These videos have been up since 2009, and I can accurately assure you that none of these people have done a single thing to *save the world* except in their own deluded ego fantasies. This is not to say that ground crew is here to save the world, or ever was. That idea in itself is also part of what storytelling does to induce internal ego fantasies and misinterpretations through human cognitive filtering processes. Such ideas spread like a meme. (See *Virus of the Mind: The New Science of the Meme* by Richard Brodie, 2004) I use these video introductions to illustrate exactly how the virus infected human mind can blow up the ego's sense of self-importance if you only give it an idea that it can relate to itself and inflate its own sense of self-importance.

The individual does not push themselves to understand what seems out of their reach with these enigmatic concepts, they instead work to condense and compartmentalize and fold them into their pre-existent belief boxes. Oh, we have this new term, 'ground crew', and based on my own ego's sense of self-importance and my mystical belief system, I *must* be part of ground crew. Yeah, that's it, *I'm ground crew!* And thus a new idea is folded into the belief box without any understanding about what the term meant, but it makes their ego feel good, and important and *special,* so the individual buys the self-induced lie based on a faulty internal rationalization process that puts them in the role of the hero here to save the world. I can think of no better example than the one provided to make my case about this internal illusion-making by the false ego. As the video clearly illustrates, this ego fantasy reached worldwide, and many people bought into their role as special 'ground crew' saviors of the world. This is what herd mentality and ego infatuation does to people.

I am also using this example to illustrate the faulty rationalization process used by the ego to shape our inner world of illusion because it works the same in everyone. You are not exempt from this type of internal rationalizing process because it is a profound symptom of the hive infection used to protect its inner ego domain and its dominance over your consciousness. I will discuss this in greater depth in another chapter, but when I get to that chapter, keep what you observe in these videos as a prime example of how the internal rationalization process is a powerful weapon of your inner ego enemy.

What we did in the war out there is no longer applicable within the human domain where fighting this war for the freedom of consciousness is concerned. The battleground now is your own inner landscape. All the books we produced are your weapons to overcome your own inner adversary and its concocted world of illusion. Each book we produced attacks an area of false perceptions of reality. We must each clean the slate of the virus inner habits and self-induced lies to find our ultimate cognitive freedom. This is your battleground, not galivanting around the stars seeking to wage a war that has already been won and is no longer an issue.

The problem with stating this plain pragmatic fact is that the mystical-minded expectations about this process have no ground to rest upon. Even in the face of this fact, it will be rejected by any and all who still insist on engaging in these mystical fantasies as a reality in their inner world of illusion and mystical desires. Their own ego belief systems, created by untold generations of mystical and supernatural infatuation, will not let go of the fantasy, and these sobering facts will fall on deaf ears. Our books have provided a process of cleaning that slate of false expectations by providing all the evidence necessary for the individual to start cleaning their own internal blackboard of these mystical and supernatural lies. As I have stated in other works, to erect a new building, the old one has to be bulldozed to the ground, and that means facing and releasing all these internal illusions, not only the illusions about the outer world, but the deeper illusions that populate our inner landscape.

The problem we encounter with our own consciousness with the storytelling mentality that is installed in our species is that it keeps us perceiving only on the surface of our awareness. I have little doubt that, when people read our books, they are looking for the latest addition to a continuing story line. I have discussed the fascination with the 'news', and how news was sought in the past by people generally living in isolated settings and only learned anything about the world around them from travelers who came from outside. This fascination on new information also included the bringing into these settings new stories, and people would sit around campfires or in inns sharing new stories with one another.

As a result of this hunger for new things, people approach any engaging new material in the most superficial manner. They want to hear the story or read the new information – they want the excitement brought about by the new. Most of the time when one reads a book, they are finished with it, believing that reading it one time gives them all the information necessary to understand what was written in the 'story'. To many, I have little doubt that books like the *WANA* books are just viewed as stories to feed the imagination of people who have a UFO fascination and have compartmentalized their ideas about such things into a box of conclusions already formed on such matters. I doubt that many readers of those books did the in-depth research that is possible by reading the links posted in the books for more enhanced comprehensive understanding of the stories, but simply read the books, compartmentalize the information superficially, and moved on to the next new data that feeds their confirmation bias.

The human hunger for the new prevents our species from dwelling on too much in depth. We are too busy chasing the next thrill to pause and contemplate the information that can bring us more profound insights. We are not a deep thinking or deep perceiving species. Everything about our cognitive awareness is very superficial and self-gratification oriented. If it feeds the ego its illusions, then that is the only purpose that reading anything garners – immediate self-gratification and framing superficial ideas without pondering the deeper implications that such information may bring us. We are a species of *thinkers*, not contemplators. Thinking like a human fulfills our hunt for the thrill and also engages our internally fantasizing ourselves as the hero. Contemplation brings us the sobering 'oh shit' moments where the false reality is shattered.

It is in facing and *accepting* these shattering moments of realization that we attack the false illusionary world of the hive ego. It is in rejecting these moments of realization and denying them, going through the internal process of rationalizing the truth away, where the ego virus defeats us the most. The goal of the ego is to protect its illusionary cognitive status quo, to maintain the false cognitive resonance that supports our inner lies. So, we more often choose to create a new, rationalized inner storyline to protect our belief illusions rather than face and accept the truth that will free our consciousness from the lies.

If you want to advance your consciousness you are going to have to outgrow the storybook mentality that drives your perceptions and how you reach your conclusions about yourself and the outer world. The ego lies to us and fills our heads with its stories all the time. It feeds us illusions about our self-importance, or about our victimhood, or our false sense of arrogance and superiority, and we continue to buy these lies about ourselves because we keep believing the stories the inner ego demon feeds to us. The virus is dead, but its habits remain, and that is your battleground, to remove the residual cognitive habits programmed into you by the virus to keep its illusionary world in place.

The purpose of this chapter is to point out this cognitive storytelling we all do to ourselves to support our inner illusions about who we think we are as governed by the ego habits and discovering who you really are absent these storied illusions. You are each going to discover these storytelling fantasies if you dig deep enough into your own inner psyche to challenge them. It is almost impossible to see this inner storytelling by the ego unless someone points out that we are doing it at all. It is such an ingrained habit of the virus that it completely escapes our notice because we have been doing it ourselves our entire lives and we don't recognize it for what it is. It is so subtle, and we do it with such ease out of daily practice that we would never even think of it as the pernicious habit of mind control that it is. It is an invisible habit unknown to all. At least now you know what to look for, whereas before this chapter you wouldn't have given it a second thought.

11. What is Limited Thinking?

"The mind is everything. What you think you become." --- Buddha

For those who have read our works or listened to our podcasts, you have heard me use the term limited human thinking plenty of times. I am going to take this opportunity to delve into the deeper meaning of this terminology because it holds high relevance to what you are seeking to achieve in finding your cognitive freedom. I am going to use a passage from Nietzsche's *Thus Spoke Zarathustra* to launch this segment, because with this passage he hits the nail on the head. Before presenting this passage, however, I must let the reader know that Nietzsche was a very prolific writer and I have not read everything he ever wrote. To be honest, I haven't even read most of it.

In my writing I am often guided to find passages in his work through the course of my research based on what I call internal 'tweaks' to look things up. I will explain these tweaks in a bit more detail later, but for now, I wanted the reader to realize that I did not depend on Nietzsche to formulate my knowledge any more than I relied on don Juan or any other source as the primary shaper of my perceptions. In most cases, I am able to translate these other writer's works and stories because I have gone down a similar path to *see* what they *see*. They often serve as sources to validate my own perceptions to others who require secondary sources before they can accept any new idea. Having cleared the air on this aspect of my writing and perceptions, the following section from *Zarathustra* is entitled *The Three Metamorphoses*:

"Three metamorphoses of the spirit do I name to you: how the spirit becomes a camel, the camel a lion, and the lion at last a child.

Many heavy things are there for the spirit, the strong weight-bearing spirit in which reverence dwells: for the heavy and the heaviest are what its strength longs for.

What is heavy? so asks the weight-bearing spirit; then it kneels down like the camel, and wants to be well loaded.

What is the heaviest thing, you heroes? asks the weight-bearing spirit, that I may take it upon me and rejoice in my strength.

Is it not this: To humble oneself in order to hurt one's pride? To let one's folly shine in order to mock one's wisdom?

Or is it this: To desert our cause when it celebrates its triumph? To climb high mountains to tempt the tempter?

Or is it this: To feed on the acorns and grass of knowledge, and for the sake of truth to suffer hunger of soul?

Or is it this: To be sick and send away comforters, and make friends with the deaf, who never hear what you wish?

Or is it this: To wade into dirty water when it is the water of truth, and not repelling cold frogs and hot toads?

Or is it this: To love those who despise us, and give one's hand to the phantom when it is going to frighten us?

All these heaviest things the weight-bearing spirit takes upon itself: and like the camel, which, when burdened, speeds into the wilderness, so the spirit speeds into its wilderness.

But in the loneliest wilderness the second metamorphosis happens: here the spirit becomes a lion; it will seize freedom, and become master in its own wilderness.

Here it seeks its last master: it will fight him, and its last God; for victory it will struggle with the great dragon.

What is the great dragon which the spirit is no longer inclined to call Lord and God? "Thou Shalt," is what great dragon is called. But the spirit of the lion says, "I will."

"Thou Shalt," lies in its path, sparkling with gold - a beast covered with scales; and on every scale glitters a golden, "Thou Shalt!"

The values of a thousand years glitter on those scales, and thus speaks the mightiest of all dragons: "All the values of all things - glitter on me.

All values have already been created, and all created values - do I represent.

Truly, there shall be no 'I will' any more. Thus speaks the dragon.

My brothers, why is there need of the lion in the spirit? Why is it not enough the beast of burden, which renounces and is reverent?

To create new values - that, even the lion cannot yet accomplish: but to create itself freedom for new creating - that can the might of the lion do.

To create itself freedom, and give a holy No even to duty: for that, my brothers, there is need of the lion.

To assume the right to new values - that is the most formidable assumption for a weight-bearing and reverent spirit. Truly, to such a spirit it is a theft, and the work of a beast of prey.

It once loved "Thou Shalt" as its most sacred: now is it forced to find illusion and arbitrariness even in the holiest things, that it may capture freedom from its love: the lion is needed for this capture.

But tell me, my brothers, what the child can do, which even the lion could not do? Why must the predatory lion still become a child?

Innocence is the child, and forgetting, a new beginning, a game, a self-propelling wheel, a first movement, a sacred Yes.

For the game of creating, my brothers, a sacred "yes" to life is needed: the spirit now wills its own will; the one who had lost the world now attains its own world.

Three metamorphoses of the spirit have I told you: how the spirit became a camel, the camel a lion, and the lion at last a child. - Thus spoke Zarathustra.

I trust the reader can see that what these passages highlight is not philosophy. It is how we live as a species. We are the camel that has taken on all the burdens of things loaded upon us by the world in which we live. It is the dragon of the ego covered with thousands of years of Thou Shalts that feed our obedience to authority syndrome and keep us from our true freedom. As is stated, every Thou Shalt has been calculated to the Nth degree where our entire perceptual world of illusion can be controlled at every turn. After eons of the hive virus tyrannizing material beings across the cosmos, our consciousness is entirely corralled. No matter which direction we turn in this corral we find the pre-existent Thou Shalts barring every gate to freedom. This is the world of limited thinking and limited perceptions.

We live in a hearsay reality where we are instructed to obey authority, to follow the herd, to comply with traditional, cultural, religious, political and legal mandates. We require the burden of obedience because we can't think or do for ourselves. We do not know how to be free any longer. The last freedom any of us tasted was when we were a child who had not yet become a member of the herd, where our imaginations could create worlds of possibilities – until that was all taken away from us. Once we became members of the herd, as don Juan stated, we become just another cow in the herd of human cattle. Obey is the watchword which we all adhere to for guidance. We know no freedom. We only know obey and submit. We must each conquer that great dragon that lies within us with its multitudes of programmed scales to find our freedom. Only one who has gone through this process can understand the story Nietzsche tells here in allegory, yet this tale is the sad truth of human existence with its limited thinking world.

Wherever you look in the outer world you find restrictions, the resounding No of the dragon. When you look at your inner landscape you are going to find yourself bound even more tightly by these inner No's. Wherever you look while seeking to clean your inner abyss you will find your individual restrictions at every turn. We have each had our habits controlled by the illusionary world of the virus. We are so subliminally programmed by the scaly green dragon we perform its installed habits and never know we are doing its will instead of exerting our own. These habits are deeply etched in the stone of our bodymind and our psyche. We cannot wipe these etchings away because they are too deeply ingrained. Our only solution is to sandblast them away by destroying them all to get to a clean base from which we can launch the creativity of the child as a genuine creator.

As human history has shown by its repeating errors, every presumed Band-Aid solution to every human ill is only another calculated and predictable scale on that dragon and his Thou Shalts. We are creatures of habit, but the cognitive mental and emotional habits we control ourselves with are *its* habits, not ours. Even our perceptions of freedom are a tacit lie. We perceive freedom as not being restricted by laws or by the word of God while complying with them completely. We even view our subjugation as freedom while we bend our knees at the altars of the law and our preferred image of God. Submission is freedom under these conditions. Yes! Give us freedom!

When you start plumbing the depths of your own inner abyss to challenge your own ego, find out how many of its No's you encounter at every turn. I can't, I won't, I shouldn't, is all you will find. These are your personal Thou Shalts. When you find these inner No's, then your questions should automatically challenge the ego with 'why not'? Why do I believe and accept this No? Who told me to believe it? Is it a decision I reached on my own, or were there other factors that programmed this No into me? Did I program this No into myself with the help of the ego to bolster its self-image? What is the *motive* behind keeping the No in place? Is the motive to make myself feel good to bolster my ego's self-image, to make my ego feel self-righteous and justified and self-important? Finding the *motive* to your No will reveal itself as an ego program if it brings up any resistant inner emotion with the challenge.

When you talk about emotional reactions people generally perceive such reactions to be like the external exhibitions of anger or joy or whatever. Emotions are also very subtle. They do not require explosive outbursts to keep us enslaved as mechanisms of the ego to feed itself. Some emotions on the inner landscape can be almost like a whisper, but they are still emotional reactions. The virus learned how to live off the crumbs of emotion, so any idea you may have that the emotions must be dynamic in their exhibition is in error.

Another mistake people make is with the faulty assumption that they are only looking for negative emotions, but emotions that make the ego feel good are equally as programmatically dangerous. The ego will deceive us by making us feel good, especially when it can make the ego feel smug or superior to others. Once again, if you discover these feel-good emotions, you must get to the root of the *motive* behind why they make you feel good. Are these feel-good sensations bolstering the inner self-image of the ego? Only by questioning your inner motive behind the feelings will you discover if they are just a food supply for the ego or not.

The ego erects protective walls around its food supplies. It arms these protective walls with emotions to ensure that you don't take these walls down that protect its inner realm of self-illusion. Don Juan challenged Castenada on more than one occasion to rid himself of his own self-importance. Self-importance is the realm of the ego. It is its realm of protected ego turf in your psyche and it uses your emotions against you mercilessly to keep its own self-importance firmly ensconced in your psyche.

As a human being you should have nothing to defend except your personal safety, yet the virus ego has everything to defend because its world is illusion. Shatter the illusion at any place and the ego loses that self-importance and you deliver a blow against the dragon for your freedom. This is why I did the podcast about having nothing to defend. This is why don Juan taught that to advance one's perceptions one must have nothing to defend, especially if they stepped into the hive *nagual* arena to do battle, for that point of defensiveness would be turned against you by that ego hive demon inside you. Having positions to defend - causes, crusades, jihads, political or religious ideologies, and especially self-image; they are areas the ego defends vehemently. If you still embrace any of these things to defend, the ego will fight you mercilessly with your own emotions to prevent you from releasing them and tearing down its walls of control. In *Beyond Good and Evil*, Nietzsche expressed it this way:

"146. He who fights with monsters should be careful lest he thereby become a monster. And if thou gaze long into an abyss, the abyss will also gaze into thee."

I have read a number of philosophers who have speculated on what they think this passage means about the abyss gazing into you. Without understanding the hapiym virus and the false ego it produced they can reach no full understanding of the passage.

Whenever you challenge the ego, it knows you more intimately than you know yourself, so to challenge its realm of belief and illusion, it will always be staring back into you, knowing exactly how to emotionally manipulate you to keep its world in place. The ego is the monster you fight against, and if one doesn't return in victory from such encounters it can and will strengthen itself and its control over you.

With all this information are you starting to understand limited thinking and limited perception? Your every thought and belief is controlled by your external culture and your inner beliefs, and the ego's incessant No's and Thou Shalts. I don't tell you this to create defeatism or create the illusion of insurmountable hurdles. If you have chosen this journey and you have been doing the preliminary work in this process, this is the deeper knowledge you need to possess to continue your personal clearing work.

These limited perceptions in thinking are your personal boundaries in the closed mall of menu-choice reality. Each of them serves as a harness for your consciousness. The preliminary work is much easier than this deeper work. It is easier to identify the glaring programs that make us more uncomfortable because they do generate more noticeable emotional reactions. The subtler inner programs are much harder to discover and scrape away because they are so habitual that we don't even recognize them as habits. Trying to think your way through discovering these deeper programs will not do. You will have to become watchful for what stirs the more subtle emotions when situations arise that may bring these emotions to your attention. It is through being aware of these inner, more subtle emotional disturbances that you will have your greatest success in detecting these programs. To attack this with guesswork will only drive you nuts in the long run so you will have to be patient as these subtler programs get flushed out from time to time.

This work doesn't require 24/7 discipline, but it does require awareness and presence of mind enough to notice these programs when they emerge so you can analyze what stirs these emotions. It is more like being on standby and keeping your awareness attuned to such things if they arise. With a little practice in noticing these subtler programs, the work is not as difficult as it first may sound.

Between the flashlight perceptions of tunnel vision focus and the multitudes of Thou Shalts which govern our consciousness and emotions, it should be readily understandable what limited thinking and perception means. Viewed with this understanding, then the claim of living in a world of limited thinking becomes an inarguable truth. Your cognitive freedom comes when you overcome these self-imposed restrictions on your consciousness. The outer world may dictate many of these rules, but your blind acceptance of them makes you responsible for how they affect you. To not question these restrictions only leaves one an unwitting slave to their emotions and the mandates placed on us by others. Perhaps this chapter more fully explains what living in a world of limited thinking means. The limits are more restrictive and pervasive than most realize or are willing to admit.

12. What's the Upside?

At this point you must be asking what you can gain from all this intense inner scrutiny and personal housecleaning. What is this second cognition awareness you are shooting for and, is all this work really worth what you are doing? I can only speak for myself and what I have gained through my own cognitive advancement and perceptual expansion. This doesn't mean your individual results will exactly mirror my own experiences, they may, or they may even transcend how this has benefitted my life.

I have done everything I can to help others eliminate all the fascination with mystical and supernatural expectations by explaining the source of these concepts and even how they worked as avenues of the hapiym hive infection. It is because of untold generations of mystical wishful thinking that whatever expectation you may have created about second cognition awareness are probably completely wrong. You will most likely be able to increase your cognitive perceptual abilities, which might seem magical or unimaginable to those who live in compartmentalized mental boxes of menu-based illusions of reality. As don Juan said of the new sorcerers of his lineage, they could perform phenomenal feats of *perception* – not magic.

These phenomenal feats of perception come about through expanding your perceptual awareness from the limited cognition flashlight tunnel vision view of the world to a 360° perception of the world around you. For a simple comparison, you might consider a 1,000-piece jigsaw puzzle where the average person is only working with ¼ to ½ of the pieces, where with your cognitive advancement, you would be working more with the full 1,000 pieces to arrive at certain solutions. Regardless of how hard these other individuals might try to perceive the full picture of the world with only a limited number of puzzle pieces in hand, what you could accomplish *perceptually* with all the puzzle pieces (or at least a larger proportion of them), and how you could extrapolate that information into sometimes very accurate prognostications from data extrapolation, would seem like magic to their limited perceptions.

Through becoming a person of knowledge, you will have a broader and wider array of information from which to formulate insightful judgments of things you may *see*. This can be related to what don Juan said about believing being a cinch, and how *having to believe* is a more difficult task. In the first cognition world people believe what they choose from the menu choices presented to them, therefore believing is easy. Having to believe entails, as don Juan taught, taking all the available data and making a value judgment on the information at hand and having to believe what extrapolating that information leads you to perceive, or *see*. The broader your generalized base of knowledge, the more your psoyca sentience can provide triggers, or 'tweaks', of insight to perceive a panoramic view you would never perceive otherwise. These tweaks will be moments of genius, and similar insights have served as profound moments of realization, often leading to invention and creation.

As your base of generalized knowledge increases, you will possess more information from which to reassess what you had to believe previously, and form new perceptions based on new and different information that can lead to even broader insights. This is why one must be a fluid warrior. We must be willing to change our perceptions in light of new and valid information when it comes our way. I wrote a long time ago in *Demystifying the Mystical* how truth is a moving target. This explains the cognitive fluidity of a warrior. Today's perceived truth may be overshadowed tomorrow if new information comes to light that causes us to reassess our prior perceptions. We must be fluid enough in choosing what we 'have to believe' in the face of a changing landscape of information.

We live in a creation that is constantly in motion. Nothing remains static and the same for very long. One of the failings of the hive was that it demanded static rigidity in its perceptual theft because it would always be the same. It could adapt to new ideas stolen from its human hosts, but it always took that new information and rigidified it into its own pre-existent domain of limited perception. The hive mind was rigid, the human mind is not, if one can break the static habits of hive thinking. The hive collective never advanced, it couldn't, it only subsumed new information and turned it into the old hive system of perceptual sameness. The hapiym virus could never offer any kind of solutions to any problem because its solution was always the same, eternal sameness. One only needs to look at human thinking based on the virus infection to see this sameness and the static lack of motion in human consciousness, always repeating the same errors of history over and over again.

The concept of *seeing* as don Juan taught is easily understandable because humans do it all the time. We encounter it when we are wrestling with trying to understand a difficult concept and someone can explain it to us, and the light comes on in our minds and we can finally *see* or understand what we couldn't previously. The more you expand your knowledge base, the more information you have at your disposal, the more your capability to *see* in this manner will increase. Your perceptions will expand based on questions you may pose so that when you get a missing piece of information, the puzzle pieces assemble, and you *see* things in a new light. You *perceive* more than you did previously. Through the practice of becoming a person of knowledge your *seeing* skill will enhance and you become a *seer*, able to perceive things that others can't, which to their perceptions would seem rather magical by comparison to their own limited capabilities.

This may not sound as enchanting or exciting as one's mystical expectations, but a vision earned through your own diligence and practiced abilities is worth substantially more than a false vision delivered at the hands of hive cell manipulation of your consciousness. *Seeing* of this nature is not visual, as don Juan taught. It is all about *perceptions*. One's perceptions are limited by what one knows and the filtering systems they use to translate information. When one uses a limited filtering system to process any information they may run across, they then compartmentalize it mentally into the boxes of their known perceptions. In the end, through faulty and limited cognitive filters used as their basis for interpretation, they understand far less than they lead themselves to believe because their perceptions become stunted and tailor to fit their own belief systems.

Confirmation bias is a trait of the hive. Confirmation bias stands on the ground of foregone conclusions on things, and any new information must be made to conform to these pre-formed conclusions, whether the new information fits into these compartmentalized cognitive boxes or not. By insisting on translating any new data and making it fit into old boxes, you find the meaning behind the parables attributed to Immanuel in the New Testament:

> *"No man putteth a piece of a new garment upon an old; if otherwise, then both the new maketh a rent, and the piece that was taken out of the new agreeth not with the old. And no man putteth new wine into old bottles; else the new wine will burst the bottles, and be spilled, and the bottles shall perish. But new wine must be put into new bottles; and both are preserved. No man also having drunk old wine straightway desireth new: for he saith, The old is better."*
>
> *—Luke 5:36-39, KJV*

With this parable it is hoped that you can now see the relevance of becoming a person of knowledge and expanding your awareness as the 'new wine' that can't be put into old wineskins without bursting them. Where people insist on the old, the new will always be rejected. Naturally, this is not the spin that theologians put on this parable, but that is to be expected since they are supporting their religious interpretations only. At best, it is left up to the reader to determine which interpretation feels more correct.

This brings us to the next level of understanding and explanations. Many readers may have come out of the modern spiritual arena where they have heard people exclaim, 'I can resonate with that'. Most of the time such statements are about egos who *want* to believe what they are hearing and claim a false resonance with the idea because it feeds their ego belief system. Wanting to believe falls under the category of believing, not having to believe. Wanting to believe is a convenience that generally feeds one's ego desires more than anything else. It is a form of belief confirmation bias. So-called resonance in such cases is primarily an emotional reaction to an idea that feeds the ego and makes it feel good about the idea or belief it is confronted with.

I will refer you back to what you observed about the Project Camelot people all claiming to be ground crew as an example of how egos 'resonate' with ideas like that. When you can get past this emotional reliance on embracing a belief that simply feeds your ego and conquer that emotional necessity, clear perception can set in and you can *see* more clearly without your emotions driven by your ego's desires to blind you to the truth. Once you can overcome that emotional investment in such beliefs, any beliefs, you free yourself from the chains the ego uses to bend you to its desires. Your emotions are the ego's control mechanism over your psyche. There is no belief that doesn't carry with it an emotional investment to protect the belief. Every belief demands *defending* as a result of this emotionalization of it, and no matter the belief, the emotions are used to reinforce the belief. Every hot button issue you can imagine brings with it an emotional commitment to defend the belief. This is why using cell talk to uninstall as many of these emotional programs as possible brings you closer to that position of having nothing to defend, where defensiveness always resides in the realm of the ego and its control over your mind through your emotions.

Getting back on track with this chapter title, what you stand to gain with second cognition advancement is a faster thinking process as you remove the programs that serve to consume your energy and rob you of cognitive clarity. In the first cognition world of perceptions with the multitudes of 'No's' that keep our consciousness lost in the perpetual realm of useless 'what if's' and mostly pointless thinking processes (the inner dialogue), our minds operate as if they are filled with sludge. This is an honest comparison because once one moves closer to and conquers the incessant inner chatter of their minds with the inner dialogue, your mind's functions are not continually overloaded expending energy on such useless thinking and worry exercises. Just try and imagine how much more clarity of thought and presence of mind you would have without all these incessant doubts and fears running through your head all the time. Imagine your mind clear of these disabling ego habits where you can have the genuine time to *ponder* things with clarity of mind and without all the continual doubts and fears eating away at your consciousness all the time.

Speaking for myself, I noticed a profound speeding up in my thought (not thinking) processes. By removing as many of the hampering belief programs I once embraced as I could, my mind became clear enough to perceive new ideas once I was no longer constrained to compartmentalized, conclusion-based thinking and perceptions dictated by the world at large. I think anyone who makes even minimal progress in the clearing process will see these changes within themselves, even before the inner dialogue finally stills into silence.

As you clear these programs of generally phantom fears and doubts, you will no longer be plagued with the same levels of stress induced by the mental worries brought about through the ego's inner dialogue. Your emotions equalize. You don't lose your emotions, but your decisions are based on contemplative analysis more than being sparked by emotional reactivity, bringing you a profound peace of mind that one cannot even imagine while lost in the inner dialogue of the ego and its constant worry-garnering. With this cognitive shifting of gears and enhanced mental acuity we find ourselves able to digest more information for analysis in any given situation and see our way through to potential solutions or outcomes that we never thought possible before. We become more skilled *perceivers*, which is a very valuable talent where navigating the first cognition world is concerned.

By removing all the Thou Shalts imposed on us by our cultures we free our minds to *see* solutions to problems that once seemed beyond our capabilities. Without the ego sludge that slows our mind, and without restricting ourselves to the mindset where we are told 'you can't do that', or 'that's impossible', you gain the ability to find possible solutions and insights, where before you would just discount those possibilities as 'being how things are'. You lose the inherent rigid thinking of the virus habits and your mind opens to new, and often impossible sounding solutions and perceptions. The more you move into the Hinterlands of second cognition awareness and beyond, these perceptions only enhance and increase. Your perceptual world and the ability to perceive it expand and continue to do so. It is not a *goal*, it is an ongoing process of growth, so long as you stick with it.

These alterations in your perception and cognitive capabilities can be very powerful allies where navigating the first cognition world of realities is concerned. While most people seem to be fascinated with magical abilities and want to do all sorts of imagined mystical acts and deeds, the pragmatic real-life application of advanced awareness goes largely overlooked by those who insist on maintaining their mystical expectations. Regardless of what changes you see in yourself through your process to advancement, there are things you are just flat going to have to accept. You are *not* going to stop being a human being on planet Earth so long as you survive in your current form. You are *not* going to magically disappear into the 5th Dimension or Ascend to anywhere else. The first cognition world of insanity will surround you at every turn as long as it survives and as long as you have to function as a human being within that physical framework. These are given hard facts that are unalterable and the sooner you can accept this the better off you will be in putting yourself in the mindset of pragmatism required to navigate this lifetime. There is no woowoo.

Returning briefly to what Nietzsche wrote about the lion turning into the child, we need to clear up all doubt about this observation. You are not going to return to the innocence of childhood. You lived it, it's gone. What he alluded to was the unrestricted imagination we possessed in childhood. We were not fully programmed as children with the overwhelming menu of No's that the first cognition world shoved down our throats and stole the imaginative creativity we had as children. As unprogrammed children we didn't accept impossibilities. We could create entire worlds in our minds. The more No's we got programmed with, the more these worlds of creative imagination were closed to our awareness. So, when Nietzsche wrote about the lion turning into the child, he is speaking of us finding that childlike creativity that was hammered out of us. You don't have the ability to create much of anything if your mind and imagination are plagued with conclusions that always tell you, 'No, that can't be done'. As Nietzsche suggested, to shift one's awareness we have to relearn the ability to reassert the resounding 'Yes!' to reclaim our stolen childlike creativity and step into our humanity.

Both Nietzsche and don Juan observed how human life has become anti-life. The mind of the predator has made us hate our very humanity, which if you think about it, is all we have going for us in these incarnations. Both these teachers saw how humans were turned into taciturn, self-pitying beasts hardly worthy of the name human because they have been beaten so mercilessly into submission at every turn. They have exchanged what humanity they have for supernatural and mystical promises of a non-existent afterlife in woowoo lands of genuine fantasy, or they have caved in to culturally induced robotic mental slavery and have forsaken their very humanity in exchange for these mystical lies. Make no mistake, Socialism is just another religion modeled on all the older religions and it woos its adherents with similar pie in the sky promises by the State that any other religion does with mysticism. Hollow promises are still hollow promises whether provided by mystical gods or the invisible State. I suggest reading *The Psychology of Socialism* by Gustave Le Bon to have this explained in detail.

I can't begin to describe my own perceptual advancement in terms that would be understandable to most people. Try as I might, there will always be a point of disconnect where lack of experiencing such things will leave a great void of understanding. I can't tell you how I do what I can do, only that I can do it. What you must each realize is that there are certain things about this process that are generally true for everyone who works at it. What I have shared in this chapter is some of those general truths that will most likely be consistent experiences across the board for everyone. But each of us is different. We each have different talents and traits that make us individuals. I can't tell you what your individual specific traits and talents might be. Those are for you to discover as you advance yourself and figure out how you work in your body.

The modern spiritual circus did a great disservice to any ideas about cognitive advancement by turning everything into mystical bullshit calling it spirituality. They peddle a first cognition perception of Buddha's Enlightenment as a 'goal'. It could be compared to a dog telling you what it's like to be a cat. There is no experiential basis for a dog to know such things any more than it is possible for a first cognition human being to describe second cognition Enlightenment. First cognition explanations about Enlightenment are reduced to little more than propagating a fanciful notion and nothing else, and the hive programming insured there was never any understanding because it could never attain that higher state of awareness itself. It could only peddle fraudulent ideas and counterfeit ideologies.

Contrary to a lot of New Age beliefs, everyone does not and will not have the same talents, traits and abilities. We are all different, and any idea that we should all be able to do the same thing is only a shadow of the hive itself. Whatever traits you may discover about yourself, to bring them to a level of proficient usage, you are going to have to practice what you discover to see how far you can take it and whether you can hone those skills or not. Practice makes perfect.

Unlike the entitlement mentality of modern spirituality, the universe owes you nothing you are not willing to earn on your own. There are no welfare-state mystical giveaways. You have to pay to play, and you pay with your efforts to better yourself. Sitting on the sidelines simply professing one belief or another does not entitle you to anything more than being a slave holding a place on the cosmic dole line that has no payoff. This is pragmatism, but it is also reality. The alternative is living in a realm of perceptual unreality and wishful thinking.

Whatever expectations you may harbor when trying to conceive what second cognition awareness brings you, they will come up short. Every expectation in the first cognition world is poisoned with mystical expectations of supernatural powers. To the first cognition world your perceptions may *seem* supernatural, but only because of the rigid constraints imposed by that world of limited perception. I can virtually guarantee that every one of you who has pondered second cognition awareness has overlooked the pragmatic applications of it in your daily lives, being more interested in talking with aliens, angels or whatever. All expectations are tainted with the hive's mystical programming and we all fall prey to it when we create our expectations. This chapter is designed to introduce that pragmatic application of second cognition perceptual skills into your daily life as a human being. If this pragmatism doesn't fit your expected desires or you find such pragmatic application boring or too humdrum, then maybe you should just continue to chase some fanciful mystical rainbow's end. How this pragmatism is being applied on the cosmic scale will be addressed in the closing chapters of this book, and they are not fanciful either, although to first cognition limited perception they will sound that way, despite the sobering pragmatic explanations that will be provided.

13. Rationalizing versus Reasoning

We are now going to discuss what is probably the most pernicious weapon created by the virus to keep your consciousness and its false self-image in place as the ruler of your mind. This is the process of rationalizing. Rationalizing is defined as the:

> *"attempt to explain or justify (one's own or another's behavior or attitude) with logical, plausible reasons, even if these are not true or appropriate."*

There is no genuine logic involved in the rationalization process. It is nothing more than internal excuse-making. It is how the virus bends our minds to its will to keep us ever locked in its clutches of control. Irrationality is often a primary component of rationalizing. In contradistinction to rationalizing, let us now look at the definition of reasoning:

> *"the action of thinking about something in a logical, sensible way."*

Can you distinguish the difference between these principles? Rationalizing supports the realm of believing. Reasoning falls into the realm of having to believe. Rationalizing is generally emotion-based thinking and emotions aren't in the least rational. Rationalizing is how the ego uses its own twisted logic to hold one's beliefs in place in opposition to accepting factual information that shows the belief to be untrue. Rationalizing is a very pernicious weapon used by the virus habits to keep us rooted in whatever supports the ego self-image. It is bad enough when we use rationalizing to continue to embrace ego beliefs from the outside world, but it becomes a more pernicious weapon to protect the false ego and what it believes about itself in our inner landscape. The residual ego habits will spare no expense to keep us convinced that we are the false ego self-image created by the virus rather than find our cognitive freedom from these false inner beliefs and ideas about ourselves by overcoming these personal internal ego illusions about who we think we are.

Rationalizing is all about defending that false ego image and then phrasing arguments whereby we justify *its* conclusions to ourselves through a form of inner self-righteous defending how correct these false self-images are. Rationalizing is *always* tainted with emotions. This is exactly how don Juan described the mind of the predator. It adopts an idea or belief about itself, its world of illusion and its inner world about its false ego, then uses rationalizing to justify to itself that its conclusions are correct. It creates a form of internal circular logic and the conclusion always winds up defending the false ego personality. Emotions are always the exclamation point on any rationalized internal argument, although the emotions may be very subtle in nature.

I'm going to use the idea of compassion and humanitarianism as an example to illustrate this circular logic. I choose these particular beliefs because they are generally universal, and most people harbor a certain self-image about how compassionate they are and concerned with humanitarian issues. After all, who wants to be considered inhumane? Don Juan called this false inner perception about how compassionate we believe ourselves to be as *faux compassion*. Nietzsche spared no amount of well-deserved polemic against Christianity and pity and its wholesale peddling of this type of compassion through pity to the world in *The Anti-Christ*. But it is through almost 2,000 years of Christian indoctrination about compassion that most of humanity has adopted the idea that they are compassionate individuals. Herd programming disparaging anyone who doesn't adopt this form of compassion as part of themselves has been a very powerful deterrent to questioning one's own compassion. As such, we have all been systematically programmed with the idea of compassion and have adopted it as part of our false ego personality. I want to share some of Nietzsche's observations on pity, for pity is wrapped in compassion, and one should see it for what it is, not what we perceive it to be. The following passages are from *The Anti-Christ:*

> *"Pity is the opposite of the tonic affects that*
> *heighten the energy of vital feelings: pity has a*
> *depressive effect. You lose strength when you pity.*

*And pity further intensifies and multiplies the loss of strength which in itself brings suffering to life. Pity makes suffering into something infectious; sometimes it can even cause a total loss of life and of vital energy wildly disproportionate to the magnitude of the cause (- the case of the death of the Nazarene). That is the first point to be made; but there is a more significant one. The mortal dangers of pity will be much more apparent if you measure pity according to the value of the reactions it tends to produce. By and large, pity runs counter to the law of development, which is the law of **selection**.*

Pity preserves things that are ripe for decline, it defends things that have been disowned and condemned by life, and it gives a depressive and questionable character to life itself by keeping alive an abundance of failures of every type."

*"If in spite of this I have been wronged a number of times in large and small ways, it was not because of 'the will', and certainly not because of any **evil** will: I would have more reason to complain - as I have just suggested - about the good will that has wreaked no small amount of havoc in my life. My experiences give me a right to be generally mistrustful of so-called 'selfless' drives, the whole phenomenon of 'neighbour love'*

that is always ready with a helpful word and a helping hand. I think of it as an inherent weakness, as a case of being unable to defend yourself against stimuli, - **pity** *is only a virtue for decadents. My problem with people who pity is that they easily lose any sense of shame or respect, or any sensitivity for distances, that pity quickly begins to smell of the mob and is almost indistinguishable from bad manners, - that in certain circumstances, pitying hands can really interfere destructively in a great destiny, in the isolation of the wounded, in the* **privilege** *of heavy debt. I consider the overcoming of pity a* **noble** *virtue: I have written about the case of 'Zarathustra's temptation', where he hears a loud cry for help and pity tries to assault him, tries to lure him away from* **himself***, like a final sin. To stay in control, to keep the* **height** *of your task free from the many lower and short-sighted impulses that are at work in supposedly selfless actions, this is the test, the final test, perhaps, that a Zarathustra has to pass - his real* **proof** *of strength . . ."*

[Emphasis in original]

If you look at humanitarianism and compassion, they are both based in pity and purport to be 'selfless drives', and this is just another aspect of hive collective programming when you see the concepts of pity hitched to the concept of the 'greater good'. Through the concept of the greater good, an individual is lauded for sacrificing his or her life for the benefit of the herd. The cost to the individual doesn't matter, it is only the greater good of the herd that is ever at stake with humanitarian efforts. I trust you can see the hive fingerprints all over these concepts. Compassion and humanitarianism are twin concepts. One must have both, for one can't be compassionate without claiming to be concerned over humanitarian issues.

As a personal test, I ask each reader to find this compassion programming inside you and then tell yourself why this program is needless and useless and convince yourself that you are not compassionate and don't need to be, then observe the process of rationalizing that engages in your mind to convince you that you are compassionate, and should by no means let go of this part of your ego self-image. Observe the excuses that start flying in your mind as the ego habits argue with themselves on why you should never let go of that compassionate part of who you think you are. What you will observe is the rationalization weapon fly into full defense mode to talk you out of letting go of this aspect of who you think you are. For every reason you may come up with to rid yourself of this faux compassion, the inner ego will come back with a multitude of excuses why you shouldn't. This is the best real-life experience I can provide to you to illustrate the ego's phenomenal excuse-making capability in our minds to keep us locked into embracing its false self-image as ourselves.

Don Juan taught that compassion was only a mask for self-pity. Everyone who harbors any type of victim mentality is cloaked in self-pity. Self-pity is the domain of the poor pitiful hive ego who is locked in a human form and isolated from its hive collective. The programmed yearning by each hive cell to be with the collective set the foundation for this whiney self-pity and it has infected every human being with its own isolated insecurities. Although virtually everyone will flatly deny that they are wrapped in self-pity, every time an ego rises to defend itself against some presumed sleight or attack by an ideological adversary, their victimhood rises to the surface as the defense mechanism of the virus habits. They may hide their self-pity for being attacked by ego bravado and an inner sense of righteous indignation, but don't be fooled by this bravado, the virus habits are protecting the poor pitiful ego because it is being attacked. "Why are you picking on me?" Have you ever heard or used those words before? That is the cry of the ego's self-pity. How about, "Give me a break!" That is ego self-pity demanding its false self-pitying compassion. I will wager you never viewed these things in this context.

The question you may ask is how I reached these assessments. They came about through sound *reasoning,* not *rationalizing.* There is no emotion involved when sound reasoning and judgment are applied, only the observation and weight of valid perceptions. The rationalizing ego denies that it wallows in its own self-pity. Sound reasoning can see through these self-deceiving lies and reveal them for what they are.

Shifting gears, let's address this victimhood mentality of the virus infection from a different angle in regard to one's growth process. I want to share a passage from *The New Paradigm*

Trilogy book, *Embracing the Rainbow*, that addresses this issue directly:

> *"Much material has been disseminated indicating that rescue and reform will be provided by extraterrestrial beings and all humanity has to do is to meditate and wait around for magical processes to change everything for them. It would be wise not to count on it. There is a saying. "God helps those that help themselves." That is a truth to put in a dozen places to remind you to let go of the "I am a victim that needs to be rescued" consciousness. You will be helped but victims will not be rescued.* **Victim consciousness vibrates below the necessary levels to enter higher dimensions.**
>
> **Giving up victim consciousness is a personal decision. It is not an easy process.** *If you rescue, you become a victim of the rescued.* **Sympathizing with those who are locked into victim consciousness supports their victimhood and ties you to them.** *Discernment allows you to recognize the situation and at that point you must acknowledge that* **this is a situation that is of their own creation through their belief that others control their choices. This does not mean that you must ignore their plight, but does determine that**

[Bold emphasis mine]

What these brief passages focus on is that victim mentality is self-imposed and that it only the individual that can overcome this mental trap that ensnares their cognitive freedom. Sympathizing with a person lost in the victim mentality exemplifies the faux compassion we all nurture inside ourselves to support the false ego persona, both theirs and our own. Sympathizing compassion is a trap for both parties.

Transcending the victim mentality is performed only by the choice of each individual to overcome and transcend it and cannot be removed by anyone but the individual themselves. If they demand to stay a victim in their own inner world of perception, they will remain a victim. Think back to that saying by Buddha, *"The mind is everything. What you think you become."* If you persist in thinking you are a victim in your mind, then that is what you are, whether the ego's process of trying to rationalize it away fights to tell you otherwise – and you can bet your bottom dollar that it will. Denial is a major weapon in the rationalization arsenal the ego will use against you. Denial is merely the avoidance of truth. It resolves nothing. It is just another excuse used by the ego rationalization process to veer you away from the success you seek.

The habits of the virus ego are buried and often run deep below our radar of perception. We are so saturated in its habits of self-justified excuse-making that we automatically shift into rationalizing without any awareness that we are doing so. It has become our default position where we constantly go to defend ourselves, our beliefs, our words and our actions.

I chose the subject of compassion and humanitarianism because it is universal, and it is a basically innocuous topic that could be attacked without creating a lot of ego emotional resistance by presenting it. It was a safer subject area, emotionally, to use as an example than challenging a religious or political belief as the example. You must be aware that whatever you believe is going to give rise to this rationalization process to keep the ego's desires and beliefs in place. Some of your own personal work areas will be very volatile. Some will be shared issues based on cultural programming, but you are going to discover that many of these inner beliefs about oneself carry an equal amount of emotional volatility when you choose to challenge them.

The greatest spark for this inner emotional volatility arises with denial that we do the things we do. If you have ever been accused of one of your bad habits by another, the defense mechanism that springs immediately into action is the ego and its rationalization process in a rush to deny the accusation, particularly if it happens to be true. The ego gets offended for being found out and then the defensive emotional tirade starts with rationalization driving the cognitive defense mechanism every mile of the journey. The more volatile the emotional reactions you feel regarding whatever issue is being peeled back and exposed is one of your greatest personal work areas. Denying and avoiding looking into your own inner mirror to tear down the defenses of your own inner ego dragon will only leave it in control of your mind and emotions. The issue will not go away until you attack it head on and remove the programming that causes the emotional volatility and defensiveness.

If you were honest and did the exercise I proposed about challenging your perceptions about compassion, then you should have observed your own inner rationalization process and how it works. Rationalization is so subtle and has become such an integral part of our nature that we don't even know we are doing it. We just do it out of *habit* without ever realizing that it *is* a habit of the ego. Any place you find this rush to denial when it comes to questioning your own inner self-image is the ego defending itself and its beliefs and actions. Sadly, these are the areas that most people avoid looking at because they do cause so much internal emotional disruption and anxiety. We avoid the discomfort of facing them because leaving these areas unaddressed allows the ego to keep the state of cognitive resonance it demands to keep its worldview in place. When I say worldview, I don't just refer to the outer world, but also your inner world, because they are intimately interconnected and inseparable to the false ego identity.

Since we are on the subject of worldview and how the ego paints its inner world with the brush of the outer world, and how the two become inseparably one world of persistent illusion, we need to take a look at psychological projection. The following synopsis is found on Wikipedia under *Psychological Projection,* and it is accurate:

This human habit of psychological projection is also driven keenly by the rationalization process of self-justification. As stated, it is an ego defense mechanism that *everybody* uses, barring no one. Every one of you does this because the virus and its habitual protective defense mechanisms like this were programmed into every human being it infected. You are not immune, no matter how much your own process of rationalizing tries to convince you otherwise.

We use this rationalizing process to disparage 'they' or 'them', never acknowledging our own self-deceptive perfidy for the same habits of ego defensiveness. By projecting our own faults outward onto others, it gives the ego a sense of superiority and boosts its false sense of self-esteem and superiority. Each of us can readily see the faults in the opposing 'them' and what 'they do', but it's rare that any individual will accept their own actions for doing the same things. When you challenge a person in this regard, the rationalization machine kicks in and the personal excuse-making of the ego goes into defensive overdrive denying their own culpability in doing the same things. Granted, our individual failings in this regard may vary from person to person based on our own programming and behavioral habits, but the defensive mechanism of projection and rationalizing away our own responsibility for similar actions is *exactly the same* in everyone.

The ego avoids taking responsibility for these things by readily blaming others rather than owning its own actions. By blaming others, the ego alleviates itself of any culpability or guilt by having to admit it does the same things. Even before psychology was any kind of practice, Immanuel, a teacher of advanced awareness saw this ego habit and warned against it.

> *""Why do you look at the speck of sawdust in your brother's eye and pay no attention to the plank in your own eye? How can you say to your brother, 'Let me take the speck out of your eye,' when all the time there is a plank in your own eye? You hypocrite, first take the plank out of your own eye, and then you will see clearly to remove the speck from your brother's eye."*
>
> *--- Matthew 7:3-5 (NIV)*

When one finds themselves in a group herd setting of any size and they can point fingers at someone they don't like or who disagrees with their own perceptual reality, you see projection disparagement run rampant. Everyone does it to one degree or another. One only needs to look at the current political climate worldwide right now to see this rationalizing projection taking place on all sides with each faction defending their own ego's positions and emotionally attacking their opponents. Remember, the hive was a collective, so beyond the individual you must bear in consideration the defensiveness of the group or herd ego created by mob mentality. The only distinction is one of scale.

Because the field of psychology has no understanding of the origin of or what constitutes the ego self, its theoretical prognostications fall far short of the genuine cure. In the same Wikipedia reference from above, under *Theoretical examples*, we find these few examples used to explain psychological projection:

> *"Projection tends to come to the fore in normal people at times of personal or political crisis but is more commonly found in personalities functioning at a primitive level as in narcissistic personality disorder or borderline personality disorder.*
>
> *Carl Jung considered that the unacceptable parts of the personality represented by the Shadow archetype were particularly likely to give rise to projection, both small-scale and on a national/international basis. Marie-Louise Von Franz extended her view of projection, stating that "wherever known reality stops, where we touch the unknown, there we project an archetypal image"."*

Given what has been shared in this book alone, not counting all the other work we have presented about the hapiym mind virus, I think the studied reader can see where many of these explanations fall sort of the mark of understanding. The mind of the virus was very primitive, but restricting it to narcissists and borderline personality disorders, or only manifesting during political stress or personal crisis, ignores the fact that everyone uses psychological projection to protect their own inner ego image through the fraudulent rationalization process. With Jung's theorizing, all the focus is on the alleged Shadow, or dark side actions of the ego personality. Jung is only working with half the equation making the mistake thinking that if something makes the ego feel good it must inherently be good. To feed the ego with feel-good sensations still bolsters the false inner self-illusion. This is where all the hive doctrines often have their most poisonous effect over our psyche. The deceptiveness of feel-good ideologies is what keeps religious and mystical traditions thriving and feeding the ego's desires and false belief systems to find that sense of power over others; its sense of self-righteousness in its beliefs, and its superiority over others by embracing those beliefs.

Because psychologists are only in the business of keeping their clients functioning as happy cogs in their cultural milieus by ensuring their cognitive resonance, they completely overlook the seductive nature of feel-good doctrines as aspects of the ego's control over our minds. You can attract more flies with sugar than vinegar, as the adage goes.

As you navigate the labyrinth of our own inner cognitive abyss, you can't overlook those things you believe that make the ego feel good about itself and only focus on what you think are the bad or negative things, as Jung mistakenly judged.

The last part of the passage and the theory by Marie-Louise Von Franz is correct for a couple of reasons which I will clarify. When we reach the known borders of our perceptions and encounter something completely foreign to them, we create an image of what we *think* (an archetype) the new concept represents. When faced with the unknown, for instance the understanding of the second cognition, we create an archetypal mental image of what we *think* it represents, having no touchstone of understanding to comprehend it. In the face of such an unknown factor, we therefore rely on our world of defined perceptual norms to try and imagine what it *might* be, and the default perception in the case of not comprehending the second cognition is to fall back on some mystical interpretational archetype. This is a more innocent type of psychological projection because it only leads to certain areas of misperception and doesn't necessarily feed the ego beyond providing it with the self-satisfaction that it has figured out the enigma of its belief, even if it doesn't understand it.

The ego compartmentalizes this unknown second cognition concept into its box of knowns, and mysticism is the box it stuffs it into. To reach this judgment for compartmentalization is not based on reasoning as much as it is on rationalizing. The compartmentalizing is not based on reason and sound judgment, it is based on conjecture and bad cognitive filtering in order to achieve a sense of cognitive resonance by stuffing the unknown into a box of the known. Through this process we find that every ego is narcissistic in nature. Every virus-created false ego is self-indulgent. What psychology classifies a narcissist to be by its definition is only the amplified and abnormal projection of narcissism, yet it overlooks the inherent narcissism present in everyone as a symptom of the hapiym virus. Every false ego is 'me' centric, thus narcissistic in nature.

I cannot express the importance of being aware of this rationalization process used by the ego as a major weapon to maintain its dominion over your consciousness. You will encounter it time and again as the method used by the ego to talk you out of removing its influence over your mind and emotions, and if you are not keenly aware of this weapon and how quickly you default cognitively and fall into its trap based on a lifetime of habitual usage of rationalizing, you will fall prey to its wiles more times than not. Even with the awareness of this you will gain by the exercise offered in this chapter, it has become such a default habit in all of us that it takes practice to be able to detect it when it is internally employed in your mind against you. The process kicks in seamlessly and automatically, and even knowing it is there will take time to discern how often it kicks in to distract your efforts to rid yourself of this and other cognitive bad habits driven by the ego programming.

14. Proving the Inversion of Psychology

In the last chapter I illustrated how the virus ego manipulates our emotions to keep its false perceptual world and beliefs firmly in place. This world is defined by external cultural norms and varies from country to country depending on many factors, the two primary factors being traditions and religions, in my own personal opinion. Cultural tradition, because it has been an ongoing accepted cultural norm for so long, embeds very deeply in the psyche because the entirety of one's culture generally adheres to these traditional norms and the consensus pressure to conform to these norms serve as a reinforcement mechanism to perpetuate continuation of these cultural norms. Cultural norms are the hardest to override whenever new political or religious concepts are introduced from an outside invading culture. A new religious ideology may be accepted by part of the populace, but the cultural standards are still deeply rooted, and a rationalization process often takes place to harmonize old cultural traditions with the new ideology, particularly if there are apparent conflicts between the two. This is the ego 'having one's cake and eating it too'.

Religions usually come with a negative reinforcement element to keep their adherents in line with the dogma once it is adopted by or forced upon the individual. You have threats of Hell or bad Karma as just two examples used as negative reinforcement tools to force adherence to a religious ideology. In the Marxist religion, it is punishment and social ostracizing by the State that serves the same purpose as the threat of Hell or bad Karma in spiritually oriented religions. From cultural traditions and religions, political ideologies probably run a close third as an element of control over the psyche. Regardless of who you are or where you live in the world, these are three of the primary programming factors that govern your perceptual outlook on the world. They are by far not the only ones, but they will have the heaviest level of programming by the mind virus to keep you marching in lockstep with your cultural herd's group ego. If you start to run afoul of any of these programmed cultural mandates, then it can bring about inner anxiety where the virus uses your emotions to control you to keep you towing the line of your cultural indoctrination. The external herd mentality also serves as a pressure mechanism to ensure that you don't break with cultural norms and buck the system. Between the internal ego emotional manipulation of fear to remain in compliance, as well as the external cultural pressure, few indeed can withstand the pressure to change themselves. Herd ostracizing is a very powerful deterrent to individual change that challenges cultural norms.

The field of psychology is in the business of keeping the ego operating in a state of cultural equilibrium. Psychology caters to the ego as supreme without having an ounce of understanding what the false ego is. It does not know the separation of the personality of the form in conflict with the false ego erected by the hapiym virus. Although Sigmund Freud tried to break the human psyche down into three elements, none of his speculative psychology, which still rules the field with many practitioners across the planet, considers this aspect of two egos in conflict with one another for control of the body and mind. From such faulty foundations it is little wonder that the field of psychology has not learned how to effectively 'heal' or 'cure' anyone. The mandate of the field is to deal with their client's emotional issues and give them the capability to fit back in with their cultural herd programming and 'cope' with being a contributing cog in the cultural social machine. As I have stated in prior works, psychology only deals with the symptomatology of the virus infection using the virus symptoms themselves to set the baseline of functionality as the human norm without understanding the infection itself.

I realize that some readers who have studied our work probably groan when we bring up psychology, but the fact is that the road to cognitive advancement is psychological in nature. You can't escape this and harboring a distaste for the subject matter is not going to help you much in seeking understanding about yourself and how to conquer your inner adversary. I do my utmost to simplify all this for the reader's understanding, doing what I can to avoid all the unnecessary professional linguistics involved in academic psychology as much as possible to bring it down to the layman's level of understanding.

One of the first aspects I want to discuss in this chapter about psychology and one's journey to cognitive freedom is loneliness, because you are probably going to feel it one way or another somewhere along the line in this process. If we look up *Loneliness* on Wikipedia we find:

> *"Loneliness is a complex and usually unpleasant emotional response to isolation. Loneliness typically includes anxious feelings about a lack of connection or communication with other beings, both in the present and extending into the future. As such, loneliness can be felt even when surrounded by other people and one who feels lonely, is lonely. The causes of loneliness are varied and include social, mental, emotional, and physical factors.*
>
> *Research has shown that loneliness is prevalent throughout society, including people in marriages, relationships, families, veterans, and those with successful careers. It has been a long explored theme in the literature of human beings since Classical antiquity. Loneliness has also been described as **social pain—a psychological mechanism <u>meant to motivate an individual to seek social connections</u>.** Loneliness is often defined in terms of one's connectedness to others, or more specifically as **"the unpleasant experience that occurs when a person's network of social relations is deficient in some important way".***

increase feelings of loneliness, it also helped to improve their cognitive state, such as improving concentration."

[All emphasis mine]

For more information on the personal subjective phenomenon of loneliness, I recommend reading the rest of the Wikipedia page from which these passages were excerpted or read other psychological prognostications about loneliness. What you should notice from the passages above is that loneliness is usually associated with a person who is expecting or used to a specific kind or certain amount of social interface that will, when removed from that social interaction, bring on these feelings of loneliness in the individual. From the standpoint of the virus infection, feeling disconnected from one's herd is foundation enough to create an emotional feeling of isolation and loneliness within oneself and can generate a wealth of internal emotions from which the virus could feed.

When one understands the collectivized socialization demanded by the virus infection, to be cut off from that programmed mandate to be part of the herd could be devastating to a hive cell who was the odd man or woman out, cut off from their social milieus. This, in my estimation, is the root basis for feelings of loneliness, regardless of what psychologists posit for its reasons. Since psychology knows nothing about the virus infection nor its collectivist drives as a singular infectious medium, this possibility is not even a consideration as the prime factor for feelings of loneliness. Whatever events may contribute to loneliness that psychology speculates about, the isolated virus cell would find any reason to implement and activate the loneliness emotional program in its human hosts.

To understand other facets that contribute to feelings of loneliness and the negative emotions it generates within oneself, let's look at a bit of cultural history to put it into context. In more ancient civilizations, when one acted against the consensus morals or cultural conventions, they were very often exiled. Being exiled on your own without the support of your culture, and in many cases even by your family, where your name could literally be erased from history, as in the Roman Empire, being alone as an outcast was one of the harshest forms of punishment short of death. Forced isolation of this kind was considered a terrible punishment. Because exile was a normal practice in many cultures worldwide, every hive cell knew the feelings of social ostracizing by the individual who often had to rely on their cultural or tribal connections to even survive. Because any hive cell who knew these feelings could transmit all the fears associated with loneliness throughout the hive collective to all other hive cells, even if one is not lonely, they harbor an inner loneliness anxiety based on the virus memory within us.

From acts of ancient exile, we take the same principle of being alone as a form of punishment and translate it into our modern world where children who don't toe the line or act up are told to take a 'time out', separated from the other children of their herd, and again, being alone results as a form of punishment. To be alone or isolated is programmed into us as being 'bad'. Such actions, as innocent as they may seem if we are a parent enforcing a time out on our children, just adds another layer to the exile ostracization program the hive cells all harbored as part of their human programming arsenal. Ergo, being alone is bad, being part of the herd is good. It is this factor of the hive cell programming that we overlook, but it is a major contributing factor as a basis for loneliness. We are taught that to be alone is a form of punishment, and that is one reason most people can't stand being alone for very long. It is a very subliminal form of hidden hive programming, but it produced a wealth of energetic emotional food for the virus to feed upon. Because of the virus infection and this subliminal association of being alone equating with punishment, if we don't have someone who is directly doling out the punishment, the hive cell could make us punish ourselves through loneliness.

Having provided my observations on loneliness for your consideration, let's redirect this discussion where circumstances on your own path to cognitive freedom may lead you into the snake pit of loneliness if you do not stay on guard against it. I am going to use the issue of conspiracy theories to make the following points because many readers have had to face such ideas, right, wrong or otherwise, and have felt the social ostracizing associated with what happens when the consensus herd refuses to hear any evidence to support those ideas.

People live in a perceptual world where they expect things to run in a certain fashion according to acceptable consensual cultural 'norms.' Everyone generally believes this to be true, so when something comes along that disrupts this consensus perception of reality, it can be cognitively devastating to an ego personality who lives in that world of consensus perception. Introduce the idea of a conspiracy that shows the world of consensus reality to be a totally false perception and watch how quickly people deny the possibility because the ramifications, if true, are just too frightening to entertain. Everyone who has gone down the road of conspiracy research, whether they have progressed down that road far enough to see the pragmatic and factual nature of a global conspiracy beyond some of the artificially produced nonsense theories or not; to face the reality of such a conspiracy disrupts one's perception of the world. People don't want their perceptual world ripped apart. The emotional discomfort that one encounters in the face of accepting the new and broader perception of reality is devastating when one accepts it. The first response internally is fear. The fear arises because our old perception of reality now comes into question and the bottom drops out of our world. We find ourselves both cognitively and emotionally at sea, because in our old perceptual reality, such things did not exist. How do we deal with this new reality when our old-world perceptions crumble?

The simplest thing to do in the face of such reality-shattering information is to call the information crazy and the person who believes it crazy as well. Denial of such things is the cognitive safe haven people generally default to in order to avoid having to admit the truth that would destroy their perception of reality. Because of the massive publicity campaign to damn conspiracy theories as nonsense, and because psychologists created a new form of 'disorder' to define those who believe conspiracy theories as mentally challenged, the average person will readily discount the truth and embrace the safety of their known perceptual reality by denying any conspiracy exists at all.

For the person who has dug into the truth of the conspiracy (and there is a mountainous amount of verifiable factual evidence), they take on the role of the town crier, feeling the need to awaken anyone and everyone who will listen to their narrative in their pleas to 'save the herd'. In most cases, this pursuit of playing town crier usually gets them ostracized by their friends and family, and the loneliness of isolation can set it. Being in such a position, it creates no shortage of inner anxiety when they can show the proof of their assertions and no one will listen. What they fail to realize is that the need to 'save the herd' is all part and parcel of the hive programming itself. It places the ego in the role of the hero on one hand, then allows them to fall into the role of the victim on the other hand when they are ostracized for not being believed. This combination creates all sorts of emotional disruption as one must now adjust to a shattered perception of reality as well as an inflated sense of self as the hero and the victim for being marginalized and ostracized. In some people, this isolation can send them into the depths of depression and loneliness. What an emotional feeding frenzy for a hive cell, no?

I used the idea of what one goes through when their worldview changes with conspiracy knowledge because it is highly applicable in all your internal clearing endeavors, and when one encounters and accepts these ideas, they are usually very perception shattering and emotionally disruptive. We each live in a created and carefully managed perceptual reality. The external reality contributes a lot to the internal reality of the false ego.

Disrupt any part of that reality and it starts to fall apart and one must adjust to new perceptions of reality. It is much easier to challenge external beliefs and ideas than it is to challenge our own ego self-image, but make no mistake, tearing down any major aspect of the ego's false image will create similar emotions of fear and anxiety as the ego habits work tirelessly to keep your consciousness right where it wants it. What you did with the compassion exercise is only a mild taste of the emotions and rationalizations you will face as you take on the deeper and more uncomfortable facets of the false personality. When you challenge aspects of the ego's self-image that you feel are an integral part of your identity, then you will be in a real dogfight. The more strongly held the internal self-image belief is, the more vicious the internal conflict with the ego will be.

The desire to deny or ignore uncomfortable facts is defined in psychology as a *Defence mechanisms*. For some insight into this we will look at what Wikipedia had to offer on the subject:

> *"A defence mechanism is an unconscious psychological mechanism that reduces anxiety arising from unacceptable or potentially harmful stimuli.*
>
> *Defence mechanisms may result in healthy or unhealthy consequences depending on the circumstances and frequency with which the mechanism is used. In psychoanalytic theory, defence mechanisms are psychological strategies*

brought into play **by _the unconscious mind_** to **manipulate, deny, or distort reality in order to defend against feelings of anxiety and unacceptable impulses and to maintain one's self-schema or other schemas.** These processes that manipulate, deny, or distort reality may include the following: repression, or the burying of a painful feeling or thought from one's awareness even though it may resurface in a symbolic form; identification, incorporating an object or thought into oneself; and **rationalization, the justification of one's behaviour and motivations by substituting "good" acceptable reasons for the actual motivations.** In psychoanalytic theory, repression is considered as the basis for other defence mechanisms.

Healthy persons normally use different defences throughout life. An **_ego defence mechanism_** becomes pathological only when its persistent use leads to maladaptive behaviour such that the physical or mental health of the individual is adversely affected. Among **the purposes of _ego defence mechanisms is to protect the mind/self/ego_ from anxiety or social sanctions or to provide a refuge from a situation with which one cannot currently cope."**

[Bold emphasis mine]

Here again, psychology does not draw any distinction regarding what the ego is, it is simply accepted without examination. Psychologists observe the symptomatology of the virus and use it as an accepted norm when reaching these conclusions about ego defense mechanisms. Through behavioral studies, psychologists have observed many habits of the false virus ego and its defenses as well as its adaptability to rationalize all sorts of excuses in our minds to protect its illusionary domain of perceived reality. When we read these passages and the psychologists talk about people not being able to deal with 'reality', we must necessarily ask the question, who defines 'normal reality'? You see, the consensus perception of reality is what is regarded as normal and is used as the measuring stick that everyone should conform to. In this case, 'reality' is accepted as a norm as much as the ego is accepted as a 'norm'. Using false baselines of 'given acceptability' has kept psychologists operating in the dark as much as the regular public. Their perceptual world of illusion conforms to the consensus reality as much as anyone else, so they are ill qualified to see beyond their own 'given' norms when seeking to define mental 'aberrations' in others. The 'norm' is the measuring stick of their own consciousness and they can't see beyond it any more than the awareness of the consensus herd. Their consciousness is corralled as tightly in the first cognition world of perceptual illusions as everyone else's.

Many people are unaware that there are not many 'conservative' psychologists practicing in the field. Most of those in the field are very left leaning in their political outlook. As a result of this political and ideological bias, the field of psychology is continually expanding what they consider mental disorders and has recently classified people who believe in conspiracy theories, as just one example, of having a type of mental disorder. They have also started adding religious believers in some cases to their bible of psychological disorders, the Diagnostic and Statistical Manual of Mental Disorders (DSM). Naturally, the ever-expanding list of alleged disorders makes plenty of money for the pharmaceutical industry which must supply the drugs to allay these falsely perceived mental symptoms in many cases.

As just one example of some of the controversy that arose out of the composition of DSM-5, the following paragraph from Wikipedia under *DSM-5* reveals the following:

> *"Various authorities criticized the fifth edition both before and after it was formally published. Critics assert, for example, that many DSM-5 revisions or additions* **lack empirical support; inter-rater reliability is low for many disorders; several sections contain poorly written, confusing, or contradictory information; and <u>the psychiatric drug industry unduly influenced the manual's content.</u>** *Many of the members of work groups for the DSM-5 had conflicting interests,* **including ties to pharmaceutical companies.** *Various scientists have argued that the DSM-5* **forces clinicians to make distinctions that are not supported by solid evidence,** *distinctions that have*

major treatment implications, including drug prescriptions and the availability of health insurance coverage. General criticism of the DSM-5 ultimately resulted in a petition, signed by many mental health organizations, which called for outside review of the DSM-5."

[All emphasis mine]

As you can tell by this paragraph alone, there is a lot of chicanery going on in the field of psychology and the pharmaceutical companies, who have a vested interest in peddling their psychoactive drugs, had a profound influence in the continual expansion of so-called mental disorders. The DSM manuals only continue to grow in size as more issues are determined to be mental disorders that very often follow a Marxist left leaning ideological agenda. Under the expanding list of defined mental disorders, it won't be long before everyone can be classified with one disorder or another, if we are not already there. Orwell's 'Big Brother' is casting a broad shadow with the field of psychology and the pharmaceutical companies leading humanity into Huxley's *Brave New World*.

By placing the defense mechanism in the realm of the unconscious mind, psychologists are also missing the fact that the unconscious mind that is driving all these defenses has been heavily poisoned by the virus infection and its habits. It was the residence of the virus ego infection. The studies by Boris Sidis, which I have provided in earlier works, fully identifies and describe the traits and characteristics of the virus unconscious mind. I will not cover those studies in this book again but refer the reader to Chapter 3 of my book *The Psychology of Becoming Human* where Sidis' explanations are shared in full.

In order for one to continue with the deeper work on this process of cognitive housecleaning, they must understand the arsenal of the virus habits to combat them and ultimately overcome them in themselves to win this war for your mind. Every small battle is a victory in this process. Every virus habit program addressed and removed, as don Juan taught, has a cumulative effect that, over time, can yield phenomenal results in one's perceptual awareness. Where people get fatigued in this process is when they expect dynamic, earth-shattering occurrences in this process. They create expectations that are often not met regarding such dynamic occurrences. While someone is hooked into chasing these false expectations, they often overlook the progress made from smaller victories, or they soon forget about them. This process of cognitive housecleaning is a *process*, not a goal.

What every person involved in this process is taking on is an eons-old Goliath that seems undefeatable. The purpose of this book is not to overwhelm you with the size and wiles of this cosmic Goliath's programs and habits, but to instruct you that, even as the boy David slew his Goliath, you can equally slay this one, provided you don't give up on yourself in the process. Because all of us have been heavily programmed with the mindset that we are somehow lesser beings, defaulting to a mental position of defeatism in this process occurs quite frequently in people. This is just another installed virus habit that can be overcome. This defeatist attitude will not work in your favor in the long run. It will lead you to frustration, sometimes depression, when we don't feel we are making progress as fast as we think we should or when our false expectations aren't met.

With our instant gratification culture and inherent human impatience to want everything and want it now, you will only drive yourself to continual bouts of disappointment when your impatient expectations aren't met. Because of this lesser-being mentality, it is easy to cave in and quit, believing you aren't making progress when that progress is not dynamic enough for your ego expectations and in your face. This is why I instruct people to *remember where you came from* – where you started in this process and how you were before doing any of the work. It is only with periodic retrospective analysis that you will see the fruits of your labor. Your progress may come in small increments, but they do add up over time and you *will* see a difference if you are sincere in your efforts and you don't let your ego's habits of rationalization deceive you in the process.

Each individual is loaded to the gills with virus programming. Your body is like a mainframe computer filled with computer viruses, and you are in the process of detecting those viruses and removing them from the mainframe. It will be hard to load new programs onto the mainframe when viruses eat up all your personal storage capacity, but for every program you remove, it creates more space for new software to take the place of the old virus software. Through the cumulative effects of virus program removal, one day things will shift for you. You can't force this cognitive shift into occurring no matter how hard you try. There is no way to tell from one person to the next which program removal will be the one that puts you over the line into advanced perceptual awareness. I have written before, and say here again, that there is no magic wand, one-size-fits-all solution to anyone's process toward cognitive growth.

Each person carries their own personal beliefs, prejudices, fears, guilt and shame based on all the events in their life. Two people being in the same place at the same time having an experience will likely interpret the experience differently based on their own prior experiences, beliefs and programmed perceptions. What I am sharing in this book is the psychological mechanisms that are generally true for everyone in identifying the virus habits that work against them in this process. Your own personal issues, whatever they may be, are not going to be the same as mine or anyone else. They are *your* personal experiences and biases and they establish your own personal filtering system of interpretation. In psychology, this is referred to as one's schema. Under *Schema (psychology)* at Wikipedia we find the following definitions and explanations:

> *"In psychology and cognitive science, a schema (plural schemata or schemas) describes a pattern of thought or behavior that organizes categories of information and the relationships among them. It can also be described as **a mental structure of preconceived ideas, a framework representing some aspect of the world, or a system of organizing and perceiving new information. Schemata influence attention and the absorption***

of new knowledge: people are more likely to notice things that fit into their schema, while re-interpreting contradictions to the schema as exceptions or distorting them to fit. Schemata have a tendency to remain unchanged, even in the face of contradictory information. Schemata can help in understanding the world and the rapidly changing environment. People can organize new perceptions into schemata quickly *as most situations do not require complex thought when using schema, since automatic thought is all that is required.*

People use schemata to organize current knowledge and provide a framework for future understanding. Examples of schemata include academic rubrics, social schemas, stereotypes, social roles, scripts, worldviews, and archetypes. "

[All emphasis mine]

To expand on this concept of schema, we must lookup *Self-schema* at Wikipedia for more personalized understanding"

*"The self-schema refers to **a long lasting and stable set of memories that summarize a person's beliefs, experiences and generalizations about the self,** in specific behavioral domains. A person may have a self-schema based on any*

*aspect of himself or herself as a person, including physical characteristics, personality traits and interests, **as long as they consider that aspect of their self important to their own <u>self-definition</u>.***

For example, someone will have a self-schema of extroversion if they think of themselves as extroverted and also believe that their extroversion is central to who they are. Their self-schema for extroversion may include general self-categorizations ("I am sociable."), beliefs about how they would act in certain situations ("At a party I would talk to lots of people") and also memories of specific past events ("On my first day at university I made lots of new friends")."

"The term schematic describes having a particular schema for a particular dimension. For instance, a person in a rock band at night would have a "rocker" schema. However, during the day, if he works as a salesperson, he would have a "salesperson" schema during that period of time. Schemas vary according to cultural background and other environmental factors.

Once people have developed a schema about themselves, <u>there is a strong tendency for that schema to be maintained by a bias in what</u>

they attend to, in what they remember, and in what they are prepared to accept as true about themselves. **In other words, the self-schema becomes** *self-perpetuating.* **The self-schema is then stored in long-term memory, which both facilitates and** *biases the processing* **of personally relevant information.** *Individuals who form a self-schema of a person with good exercise habits will then in return exercise more frequently.*

Self-schemas vary from person to person because each individual has very different social and cultural life experiences. *A few examples of self-schemas are: exciting or dull; quiet or loud; healthy or sickly; athletic or nonathletic; lazy or active; and geek or jock. If a person has a schema for "geek or jock," for example, he might think of himself as a bit of a computer geek and would possess a lot of information about that trait. Because of this, he would probably interpret many situations based on relevance to his being a computer geek.*

Another person with the "healthy or sickly" schema might consider themselves a very health conscious person. Their concern with being healthy would then affect everyday decisions such as what groceries they buy, what restaurants they frequent, or how often they exercise. Women who are schematic on appearance exhibited worse body image, lower self-esteem, and more negative mood than did those who are aschematic on appearance."

[All emphasis mine]

These passages illustrate the factors that are used by individuals to frame their ego's false self-image. One's personal schema is often the fiction of the ego self. Given this awareness of schemata, then I think the reader should clearly see what I mean when I say you don't know who you really are. As noted above, people change their schema masks to present themselves in different manners to different audiences (the rock musician at night, the salesman during the day). All of us change our personal schemata to present ourselves to different people how we want them to perceive us for ego acceptance in any given circumstance. This should illustrate the shallowness of the ego false identity, i.e. *it is highly inconsistent.* The virus didn't know who it was because it was just a recording device, but because it could tap into the memory of the hive database collective, it could draw on any schema necessary to put forth whatever self-image propped up its own illusionary self for the consumption of others. It then programmed these various fake roles into our consciousness and embedded them for long term usage as *its* habits.

As don Juan taught, we live in a world of definitions, and the definitions we apply to ourselves at the behest of the ego virus further sustain that world of definitions. When you do your internal deprogramming of virus habits and beliefs you embrace about yourself, you are going to have to question *why* you believe what you believe about yourself. Is what you believe to be you *really you*, or is it just a definition, a mask adopted by the ego to sustain its inner world of illusion that made you believe that *it* is you? Wherever you find aspects of this phony ego-self masquerading as the real you, you are also going to encounter emotional resistance to challenging it, so be prepared.

Ideally this chapter has helped further identify the nature of your inner adversary. Even with the overviews offered in this chapter, the reader is invited to inquire deeper into any of these areas of interest for your greater understanding. There is more to come in the next chapter.

15. Compartmentalization

As presented in the last chapter, the ego employs psychological defense mechanisms to protect its false self-image. One of the methods it uses is compartmentalization. The following short excerpts come from Wikipedia under *Compartmentalization (psychology):*

> *"Compartmentalization is a subconscious psychological **defense** mechanism used to avoid cognitive dissonance, or the mental discomfort and anxiety caused by a person's having conflicting values, cognitions, emotions, beliefs, etc. within themselves.*

> *Compartmentalization allows these conflicting ideas to co-exist by inhibiting direct or explicit acknowledgement and interaction between separate compartmentalized self-states."*

> *"Psychoanalysis considers that whereas **isolation separates thoughts from feeling, compartmentalization separates different (incompatible) cognitions from each other**. As a*

secondary, intellectual defense, **it may be linked to rationalization**. It is also related to the phenomenon of neurotic typing, whereby everything must be classified into mutually exclusive and watertight categories."

"Compartmentalization may lead to **hidden vulnerabilities in those who use it as a major defense mechanism**.

Those suffering from borderline personality disorder will often divide people into all good versus all bad, to avoid the conflicts removing the compartments would inevitably bring, **using denial or indifference** to protect against any indications of contradictory evidence.

Using indifference towards a better viewpoint is a normal and common example of this. It can be caused by someone having used multiple compartment ideals and having been uncomfortable with modifying them, **at risk of being found incorrect**. This often causes double-standards, **and bias**."

"Conflicting social identities may be dealt with by compartmentalizing them and dealing with each only in a context-dependent way."

In all honesty, what I have presented is the lion's share of information about compartmentalization on Wikipedia. As you will note, the psychoanalytic perspective denotes extreme cases of compartmentalization in borderline personality disorders. Yet, everyone compartmentalizes cognitive areas of discomfort to avoid facing those unpleasant aspects we don't want to face about ourselves under the effects of the virus. Also pay attention to how compartmentalization is associated with rationalization.

To illustrate how the field of psychology micro-analyzes certain cognitive and emotional concepts to death by labeling them, we will now look at *Isolation (psychology)* on Wikipedia to gain further understanding of compartmentalization:

> *"Isolation is a **defence mechanism** in psychoanalytic theory first proposed by Sigmund Freud. While related to repression, the concept distinguishes itself in several ways. **It is characterized as a mental process involving the creation of a gap between an unpleasant or threatening cognition, and other thoughts and feelings.** By minimizing associative connections with other thoughts, the threatening cognition is remembered less often and is less likely to affect self-esteem or the **self concept**."*

> *"As a defense against harmful thoughts,
> isolation prevents the self from allowing these
> cognitions to become recurrent and possibly
> damaging to the self-concept."*

[Bold emphasis mine]

Isolation occurs when we isolate those thoughts, memories or ideas that cause unpleasant emotional responses in ourselves. We isolate the unpleasant memories that trigger negative emotional feedback, and in some cases totally repress the memories as too emotionally challenging to face. This occurs with cases of extreme trauma, but a trauma doesn't have to be extreme to create compartmentalization of isolated uncomfortable cognition functions associated with emotional responses. Fear is the primary defense mechanism used by the ego to keep us in line, and by denoting fear as the most powerful inhibitor to protect the virus ego's self-image, we must view it in its other permutations as guilt and shame, as well as the lesser aspects of fear – embarrassment or sheepishness. The latter two aspects can be easier to overcome than the more severe fear programs such as guilt or shame.

In all cases, it comes down to protecting the self-image of the false ego personality. When one can transcend all these programs they realize they have nothing to defend where protecting their self-esteem is concerned. Self-esteem is only the self-gratification and validation program of the false ego. So now we need to look at what *Self-esteem* is at Wikipedia:

*"Self-esteem is an individual's subjective evaluation of their own worth. Self-esteem encompasses **beliefs about oneself** (for example, "I am unloved", "I am worthy") as well as emotional states, such as triumph, despair, pride, and shame. Smith and Mackie (2007) defined it by saying "The self-concept is **what we think** about the self; self-esteem, is the positive or negative evaluations of the self, as in how we feel about it."*

Self-esteem is an attractive psychological construct because it predicts certain outcomes, such as academic achievement, happiness, satisfaction in marriage and relationships, and criminal behaviour. Self-esteem can apply to a specific attribute (for example, "I believe I am a good writer and I feel happy about that") or globally (for example, "I believe I am a bad person, and I feel bad about myself in general"). Psychologists usually regard self-esteem as an enduring personality characteristic (trait self-esteem), though normal, short-term variations (state self-esteem) also exist. Synonyms or near-synonyms of self-esteem include many things: self-worth, self-regard, self-respect, and self-integrity."

"The identification of self-esteem as a

*distinct **psychological construct** is thought [by whom?] to have its origins in the work of philosopher and psychologist, geologist, anthropologist William James (1892). James identified multiple dimensions of the self, with two levels of hierarchy: processes of knowing **(called the 'I-self')** and the resulting knowledge about the self **(the 'Me-self')**. Observation about the self and storage of those observations by the I-self create three types of knowledge, which collectively account for the Me-self, according to James. These are the material self, social self, and spiritual self. **The social self comes closest to self-esteem, comprising all characteristics recognized by others.** The material self consists of representations of the body and possessions, and the spiritual self of descriptive representations and evaluative dispositions regarding the self. This view of self-esteem as the collection of an individual's attitudes toward oneself remains today."*

[Bold emphasis mine]

What we need to pay attention to in James' theory is the separation in what he calls the 'I-self' and the 'Me-self'. Psychology has still not figured out that we are talking about two distinct 'entity-selves' that have evolved into a single functioning unit. You have the personality of the human form, then you have the false identity of the ego virus. As noted, self-esteem is measured through the eyes of others, the social self. How one sets their personal self-esteem value is mostly predicated by the ego virus self, measuring itself against the herd collective consensus reality, which sets the 'values' that we all measure ourselves against for acceptance. Self-esteem is based on what we 'believe' about ourselves rather than being based on knowing who we are and our own self-worth without relying on the valuation systems of the external herds and their acceptance limitations on behavior, beliefs and morals. When one doesn't measure up to herd standards, or whose ideas stand outside those dictated herd norms, then one's ego self-esteem comes into question.

Compartmentalization also plays a role in self-esteem if we isolate thoughts or ideas that go against herd cognitive restrictions and recriminate ourselves for say, lustful or violent thoughts as examples, that go against culturally mandated norms. Because our ideas don't align with consensus reality and rules, then we can guilt ourselves over such unruly thoughts because they don't comply with herd behavioral mandates. This is but one small example of how the ego habits control us even if we are only dealing with our own thoughts and beliefs about ourselves. These secretive thoughts, which everyone has in one capacity or another, generated a lot of internal fear energies by the virus just on the idea that someone might find out our 'secrets'.

It is through this type of 'skeletons in our closets' that the virus used our emotions against us mercilessly. The fear of exposure or the embarrassment or shame at harboring such thoughts, or continually self-induced guilt or shame over something we did in the past or was done to us, serve as compartmentalized and isolated emotional control mechanisms that keep up these inner blockades. It doesn't matter what the areas of our self-beliefs on the cognitive level may be that cause this emotional discomfort, the virus habits would incite these emotional reactions within us to feed itself. Now that the virus is dead, the body still holds the memories and triggerable emotional reactions installed by the virus, and it is these habits we all seek to overcome in the clearing and growth process.

Depending on the level of emotional control we give these inner secrets over our awareness, they can become what I call *red lines* that can derail our advancement if we refuse to face them down and cross that red line. With more traumatic episodes, the memories may get repressed and we may not even be aware that our waking state memory has removed our recall of such events, but we still experience uncomfortable emotional misgivings for what seems to be no explanation.

Once we become rigid in a belief that establishes the ego's self-esteem and false image of itself, we are also facing potential red line issues that keep us rooted in first cognition perceptual reality. Most everyone has had an experience where a friend or loved one has called us down for one of our nagging habit shortcomings, and in virtually every case the ego jumps to defend itself. Under ideal circumstances we would listen to these criticisms and take them as indicators of inner work areas rather than strongly defending them. In fact, when we do get criticisms of this nature, one would be wise to pay attention to them as potential help in finding hidden inner ego programs rather than rushing to the defense of the ego.

Any time we reach one of those self-perceptions that bolsters the false ego personality that we refuse to address only leaves the habits of the virus firmly in control of our minds and emotional reactions. When people embrace these things as unalterable parts of themselves rather than addressing them and clearing the program habits, then the individual can hit one of those red lines the ego refuses to cross and their progress can not only stop, but serve as a complete inhibitor to further cognitive growth. The red line issue becomes the leash that keeps us firmly rooted in the world of ego illusions.

Although this chapter is not that long, the principles covered should add to your arsenal of understanding to see that everything presented herein is associated with defense mechanisms, including the necessity to defend one's self-image, or self-esteem. The only thing that ever required defending was the virus ego and its world of perceptual illusions. You are defending *beliefs*. This chapter has only further educated you to more clearly see the tactics of your inner adversary and how inept the field of psychology is to see through the symptoms and definitions it provides to arrive at the root of the problem. You must wonder if psychology can accept William James' concept of the 'I-self' and the 'Me-self' as separate configurations of cognition, or more accurately two separate entities inhabiting one form, why it couldn't discover the virus doppelganger? The reader is encouraged to investigate these matters further if you want more information on these subjects.

16. Constructed Reality

We are now going to push you off the high dive into the deep end of reality, into what we fondly refer to as the voodoo material. From here forward this book is going to get very curly because it is going to take you out of the realm of your normally perceived human belief system. In all honesty, I think most readers will simply balk at what follows because it just sounds too 'out there' to be real. That's why we call this kind of information voodoo and it is left to the discretion and discernment of the reader to decide whether to take it or leave it. For myself, this is the greater reality and what humanity faces in just a few short years the way things are taking shape on this planet if my assessments are correct. Be that as it may, the reader is invited to *sense* the validity of all the information and not rely on your *thinking* mind to give you the assurance of its validity.

The first thing we are going to do is utilize the movie *The Matrix* to lay a foundation for understanding. The reader must understand that humanity has been getting messages about the greater reality for a long time now, often presented through films, spiritual traditions and science fiction novels. Living in our superficial first cognition world of perception, most of us only view these messages as entertainment and never have a clue that there is something larger going on behind the scene of our limited perception of reality. The first *Matrix* movie was one of those avenues for messages to be delivered to humanity, provided one has the insights to perceive beyond the entertainment value of a science fiction action move to *see* the hidden messages in the film. Whether the reader is willing to accept this or not is up to them.

The Matrix captured the imagination of almost the entire planet since its release. Everyone who saw that movie walked away from seeing the film somehow altered. The film left a lasting impression and has had far reaching effects in the 20 years since its release in 1999. I will point out here that this is the same year that the *New Paradigm Trilogy* was published. This will have high relevance as we continue with this presentation.

I have stated in other works that Earth is a microcosmic reflection of the macrocosm of creation. What we find as a primary message in the *Matrix* film, although being a fictional presentation, is that the *Matrix* is a microcosmic representation of the multiverse at large shown in allegorical form. Although there are multitudes of clues in the movie that provide direct correlations to our 3D reality, I am not going to focus on all of them. Those who have watched any decent conspiracy videos will find no shortage of *Matrix* correlations, up to and including the addition of the term being 'red pilled' added to the common lexicon. If you have not yet watched *The Matrix*, it is strongly suggested that you do.

The Matrix in the film is an artificial virtual reality designed by a tyrannical Artificial Intelligence (AI) program that eventually enslaves all humanity. The first and hardest revelation to accept is that the fictional tyranny of the *Matrix* is only a reflection of the entire multiverse represented through allegorical means. Although creation is not controlled by machine AI, an equivalent system of tyranny existed across the multiverse where controlling the perceptions of all material beings exists, just like being plugged into the *Matrix*. This is the entire first cognition system of awareness controlled by the hapiym mind virus. What follows is going to read like a horror story to some, but there is a way out of all this, and that is what must be emphasized regardless of how grim what is revealed may seem.

Within the *Matrix* world, the heroes of the movie could replicate aspects of the *Matrix* in what they called a 'construct program'. Within the construct program, which was modeled on the same principles as the *Matrix*, anything that could be produced in the *Matrix* could be duplicated for training purposes or otherwise in the construct. Nothing that could be fabricated in the construct program could go beyond the structure of the *Matrix* it was duplicating from.

So, let's do some comparison to creation at large. The first time Neo encounters the construct program, he finds himself in an all white area with no definable features such as walls or anything that gives one any idea of the scope, range or boundaries of this blank white area. We can equate this blank white area of the empty construct to the blank slate used by the etheric consciousnesses that started the process of creating the Matrix we know as the universe of the material realities. For easier understanding of this scene, I am providing a YouTube link for the scene below:

The Matrix the Construct Explained

We must place ourselves into the minds of these creator consciousnesses and realize that they were seeking to create something out of nothing. There was no material existence from which to draw a blueprint to create the universal reality that we perceive as the cosmos and our material reality. When you can wrap your head around this concept, then it should not be that difficult to relate the clue of the white-out region known as the construct in the *Matrix* movie to a non-existent framework upon which material reality was created. It should not be interpreted as a literal comparison, but an allegorical representation of a greater truth inviting us to solve the riddle.

We must now re-examine and reassess the nature of these primary creators that started the manufacturing of material existence from their own imaginations. Contrary to popular belief that there was a singular Creator of the universe who was all-wise and all-knowing, we must trash this notion when we address it pragmatically. These consciousnesses that started the material creation ball rolling could not be all wise because they had no clue what they were about to create. The more realistic nature of their awareness could be equated in the microcosm reflecting the macrocosm concept by finding a correlation in human imagination, and that is found in the mind of a child.

Childhood imagination can create its own worlds of reality more readily than that of an indoctrinated adult. If we use this microcosm/macrocosm comparison, then we must conclude that these original creator consciousnesses had the vivid imagination, as well as the lack of wisdom in creating as a human child. Their imagination was unbounded with ideas on what to create, but there was no well thought out wisdom behind what they created as human beliefs about creator gods falsely presume. Within this framework I think you can see the hazardous downside to unbridled and undisciplined creating. This is why we live primarily in a *No Rules Multiverse* as I related in my book of the same title.

Now, let's return to solving more of the riddle clues provided in *The Matrix* movie. Within the world of the AI controlled *Matrix* we find guardians both inside the virtual reality construct as well as outside it. Within the *Matrix* we find the Agents, who can take over any virtual reality body to hunt down anyone who threatens the *Matrix*, and outside we find the Sentinel machines that search and destroy any material human beings, who are all a threat to the AI virtual reality of the *Matrix*. Using the same macrocosm/microcosm comparison between the clues in the *Matrix* and the created material universe, we must reach the realization that there are similar enforcement guardian programs built into the structure of the first cognition multiverse to keep it stable and controllable. One of the best examples of one of these types of programs was with the hapiym mind virus program. The hapiym virus was not the only guardian-type program within the multiverse Matrix, but it is the one through which we can draw our example for a general model to perceive the other enforcement programs.

What I feel I have proven beyond a reasonable doubt in all my works on the hapiym mind virus is that the virus would subsume anything new that humanity might invent with its own creativity, then twist it to the purposes of the hive program to control human consciousness. Whenever humanity tried to advance, the mind virus collective would subsume that knowledge, add it to the hive database, then adapt the infection to stultify and halt human cognitive advancement. No matter what was introduced into this paradigm across the multiverse we found the hive virus there to turn every material being back to the control mechanism of the cosmic hive Matrix. There was no exit.

I have written extensively about four teachers who I feel left the greatest impact on human consciousness, so I want to focus on a couple of them, draw a correlation to *The Matrix* movie, then expand to the multiverse at large so you can see how the clues are assembled. The person we know as Buddha is the first historically recorded individual who transcended first cognition awareness and left teachings about higher second cognition consciousness to the world. Although the first cognition collective mind of the virus functioned totally within the matrix of the multiverse, which was also first cognition perceptual reality across the spectrum, it couldn't comprehend the 'anomaly' of second cognition perception. The best it could do to subsume Buddha's teaching about higher-level awareness was to fabricate an institutional religion to shut down the teachings and keep human consciousness totally locked into first cognition awareness. About 500 years after Buddha, Immanuel started leaving similar teachings, and there was no time wasted in creating institutional Christianity to misdirect humanity once again down a first cognition rabbit hole of controlled consciousness.

The first cognition system of controlled awareness *is* the Matrix. Every human species across the entire multiverse and into creations beyond this one has been a slave to this system of limited and controlled perceptual awareness. As a correlative reference regarding what I shared above about the corrective mechanisms of the first cognition system of control, we only need to look at the scene in *The Matrix: Reloaded,* where Neo meets the architect to see the clues. Below, find two links to watch this scene. Pay close attention to what the Architect tells Neo because it has key points of relevance in the chapters to follow regarding understanding the war on consciousness, where it is going and what it is going to entail before it's over. There is more truthful information on many levels in this scene than you may at first realize.

The Matrix Reloaded - The Architect Scene 1080p Part 1
https://www.youtube.com/watch?v=cHZl2naX1Xk&t=2s

The Matrix Reloaded - The Architect Scene 1080p Part 2
https://www.youtube.com/watch?v=LN8EE5JxSGQ&t=2s

As we observed at the end of the first *Matrix* movie, when Neo rose from the dead, it created a system failure of the *Matrix* grid because such a thing was unaccounted for in the *Matrix* program as being possible. The *Matrix* had no coding to immediately compensate for the anomaly of a human being coming back from death, and because that consideration had not been factored into the guardian program of the *Matrix*, it caused a catastrophic system failure when it occurred. In like kind, when Buddha transcended the boundaries of first cognition perception and moved into second cognition awareness, the hive Matrix had to compensate for that anomaly as best it could by writing new programs to circumvent it and prevent it happening again in the future as a threat to its system of cognitive control.

Another scene in *The Matrix* that precedes this has Neo and Trinity loading up from the construct program to rescue Morpheus. Trinity tells Neo that the plan won't work because it has never been done before, but Neo explains to her that that is *exactly* why it is going to work. In other words, it was not factored into *The Matrix's* guardian program as a possibility.

To further my contention about the first cognition system of awareness having its own form of guardian programs, when the Architect told Neo that he was the sixth version of the anomaly, we find the fact that the multiverse system of human awareness also has built-in compensation programs, or 'glitch fixes' to its programming. Equivalent anomalies in our world are those found when Buddha transcended the system, as well as when Immanuel introduced similar teachings. In both cases, as with the *Matrix* films, the guardian control programs came into play, factoring in these new anomalies and subsuming them. The first cognition system of consciousness control created a self-sustaining tyranny through the hapiym virus to compensate for anything that came about *within* that system. Any new innovations, particularly where cognitive advancement was concerned, were quickly replicated, up to the point of the cognitive shift where the individual had defeated and eradicated the hive cell within. Beyond this second cognition threshold the hive could not replicate or compensate.

At the times that Immanuel and Buddha introduced their anomalies of advanced awareness into the first cognition matrix, there was no second cognition alternative realm of consciousness for humanity to step into as a viable choice to *exit* from the first cognition reality and 'escape the Matrix'. As such, just as with the construct program used by Morpheus as a training program for Neo to learn about the Matrix, their teachings were introduced from *within* the first cognition matrix and could therefore be easily hijacked and compensated for by the first cognition matrix itself. The real meaning of their teachings remains an enigma, and institutionalized religions rushed in to fill that gap and redirect people right back into the first cognition matrix of cognitive virus mind control. The way the hive compensated for what it could not understand was to create mystical and seemingly supernatural occurrences within selected human minds that were then sold to the public as philosophical, religious, spiritual and occult ideologies.

The consciousness that created the hive virus was only one of multitudes of tyrants that wrote programs onto the tapestry of the first cognition created material matrix. Not all these tyrants were immaterial consciousnesses. There were plenty of others who were material beings within the first cognition matrix who did plenty of their own damage creating more control programs from the material side of creation. I will cite Enki and Ninhursag as two of the most recent examples of more localized Earth tyrants who were both physical beings to start with. Couple them with the Orioners, who created the Anunnaki, and the list just increases for the creators of guardian programs to keep the tyranny of first cognition reality firmly rooted in place. Magnify that across the scope of the multiverse and perhaps you can start to perceive how vast and pernicious such a system of tyrannical programming reaches and how much there is to control that system of material human awareness. It's not a pretty picture to face.

Just as the computer AI controlled the perceptual reality of those human beings cocooned within the *Matrix*, the hapiym virus and its false ego program residuals control human consciousness to this day through very similar means. We live in a world of perceptual illusion insidiously fed to us through all the systems of control on this planet - education, religion, politics, sports, entertainment, the news and multi-generational programming from parents to children. Humanity's consciousness on this planet is as equally controlled as those enslaved to the AI system in *The Matrix*. Every time humanity has tried to advance its consciousness, the controllers were right there to co-opt inventions that could lead our entire species out of this first cognition abyss and turned them into tools of warfare and control, all while the hapiym mind virus kept our consciousness firmly under its control preventing that advancement.

One of the most truthful and informative scenes in *The Matrix* is when Neo finally meets Morpheus. Listen *carefully* to how Morpheus explains the matrix in the scene provided on *YouTube* at the link below. The title of the link is there for those readers who don't have direct access to the hotlink through

Kindle. Our world is much like the *Matrix* where Morpheus tells Neo that, "It is the world that has been pulled over your eyes to keep you from seeing the truth." When Neo asks, "What Truth?", and Morpheus states, "That you are a slave, Neo. Like everyone else you were born into bondage, born into a prison that you cannot smell or taste or touch. A prison. . . for your mind."

The Matrix Meeting Morpheus Scene HD
https://www.youtube.com/watch?v=gDadfh0ZdBM

What I want to point out first is in reference to Morpheus talking about 'knowing' something is wrong. This *knowing* is a form of subliminal psoyca perception that triggers us into questioning the reality in which we live. This particular scene has prompted many people around the world to start investigating the nature of their reality, even if this questioning is still being performed on the superficial levels of first cognition perception. This gives everyone a starting point to move toward advancing their consciousness so long as they don't get trapped in just another first cognition perceptual reality rabbit hole and dig in their heels to an adjusted form of perceptual belief.

The entire first cognition system of perception is predicated on *beliefs*, as I reported earlier. Within this system of control, changing beliefs can be done without one advancing their consciousness. They can go from one belief to another and still remain trapped in the first cognition system of controlled perceptions. Cognitive advancement is all about perception and a form of inner *sensing* that has nothing to do with emotional feelings. Emotions often drive these changes in belief systems because they make the individual feel good in the belief once adopted. In such cases, your emotions become part of the system of self-deception and can't be relied upon as your guide.

The inner knowing that Morpheus refers to in this scene is more about psoyca sentience working to trigger us to investigate and 'feel' or *sense* our way out of the first cognition matrix. By feel, I am referring to a form of intuitive reckoning for want of a better term, *not* emotional feelings. It is a sensory feeling unaccompanied by emotion, what some may refer to as gut instinct.

Coupled with this silent internal form of knowing that something is wrong, many people have an inner drive that 'pushes' them to keep striving to discover the truth of the illusion. It is a long and arduous process that takes time and diligence, and unfortunately, all the information we use to decipher the mystery is controlled by the same system that controls our mind. What is not wholly controlled is where we find the enigmas and the mysteries that even the hapiym hive could not compensate for beyond fabricating its 'Oneness' belief systems of control, what esotericists call the Perennial Philosophy. Regardless of the doctrinal clothing this philosophy may be wrapped in, the end point always leads one to the hive realm of false supernatural beliefs.

The hive intelligence network could never move into second cognition awareness because eradicating the virus within was the doorway that led to that level of cognitive awareness, which is why the mind virus could never hijack what it could not see beyond. This explains why most spiritual traditions mirror the psoyca path – *up to a point*. This is also why the Perennial Philosophy, regardless of its doctrinal permutations, is the same at its root, but in the end leads to a dead-end of unfulfilled spiritual promises. The so-called Perennial Philosophy is the common thread that ties all the religious, occult and spiritual hive doctrines together.

Although the virus itself is dead and gone, we all carry its programming in both our mind and bodymind. The clearing processes that we have created and offered through our books are major steps in removing these residual programs so we can progress into second cognition awareness and beyond. They are not a magic bullet, as it takes drive and a lot of fortitude to actively pursue those areas that will bring about varying levels of cognitive dissonance that break these ingrained habits and transcend them. Most people actively avoid such psychological disruption because of how its shakes our instilled belief systems to their core. Yet, painful as it is, this is the *only* way to overcome the habits of the virus so we can move into higher states of sensory awareness. This is just one more example of how the alleged science of psychology is inverted where its conclusions about curing the human psyche are concerned. Psychology steers you away from exactly what *will* cure your consciousness.

Fear is a base element of all living things used to protect our material forms from harm. What the virus did was use this base programming for self-protection and expand a survival instinct into protecting its phantom belief systems. Letting go of a belief is not life threatening, but the way the virus programmed our emotions through tampering with this basic fear instinct, it transferred this protective fear mechanism for survival and used it to protect its false world of illusion. Letting go of beliefs is *not* life threatening in the least to our physical survival regardless of the fear mechanism that will arise within you whenever you challenge your deeply held beliefs, both about the outside world and the inner world of the false ego. It is this twisted abuse of survival fear that creates the cognitive dissonance when our perceptions of the false reality and our beliefs are threatened. These beliefs are *phantoms*, yet the fear we feel is just as powerful and real as the fear used as our survival instinct. It is this type of artificial fear that don Juan called the first enemy of the warrior.

Humanity has been prompted about what awaits humanity on the horizon through many different outlets – books (factual, spiritual and fiction), TV shows and movies. Because most of humanity is lost in the first cognition world of illusion, and at best only perceives on a very rudimentary and superficial level, those who may have read these books and seen these film presentations have not extrapolated their meaning beyond that same level of cognitive superficiality. Even with the clues left in *The Matrix*, the interpretation level is only on the most basic level of awareness and few, if any, have seen the deeper clues presented in that film series and how they relate to the greater reality that lies ahead of us. A person cannot rely on first cognition beliefs and perceptions to advance beyond those perceptions. One must push themselves into territories of the unknown and listen to that inner psoyca voice of guidance when it provides us with perceptions that mainstream thinking within the first cognition world define as crazy ideas. It is when we learn to listen to and embrace ideas about the impossible that the impossible becomes possible.

17. Clues about the Shift in Consciousness

There have been rumors about a global shift in consciousness circulating for over three decades now, which really reached their crescendo prior to a prophesied date of this Shift in 2012 based on Mayan prophecy prognostications. This desire for a shift in consciousness has been capitalized on by many segments of global culture but has been more highly emphasized by Leftist movements to validate such things as the global climate change hoax presently causing unrest around the planet. The Shift idea still permeates New Age and spiritual movements with some asserting with the same certainty of the 2012 Mayan prophecy, that 2020 is going to be the new year for the shift in consciousness.

Much of what is being peddled as a shift in consciousness by the climate change and global warming crowd is not actually a shift in consciousness in the truest sense of the idea but is in fact only a shift in political perspective within the first cognition world of fantasy illusions. It is being used as nothing but a propaganda tool for herding the masses into another belief system mostly based on fear as the herding element. By calling this fear driven Leftist political fantasy a shift in consciousness, we can see the science of term co-opting and neurolinguistics at play to sell this globalist political ideology as the formerly mystical-oriented shift in consciousness. It's just a form of cognitive bait and switch.

There is no genuine shift in consciousness at play by using that term to push this political ideology, but most people who believe in a shift in consciousness scenario have no real concept of what a shift in consciousness entails to begin with to know the difference. It is simply another form of cognitive illusion based on stark ignorance and faulty beliefs.

I will be the first to admit that we are now plagued with unusual weather patterns with storms getting stronger and tornadoes appearing in places they never appeared in the past. But contrary to the global warming scam being foisted on the world population at large, these altered weather patterns are a result of weather wars that have been waged probably since the 1970s or thereafter. We have weather systems out of control because arrogant human scientists have so tampered with the natural weather cycles that they are now out of control and beyond human repair. These same scientists who have caused these weather issues are now the ones serving as the harbingers of doom over the global warming hoax, and they were the instigators of the problem to begin with. I am reminded of an old TV commercial about fake butter where we are told, "It's not nice to fool Mother Nature".

In not so many decades in the past there was no panic button being pushed about global warming. Our overly-esteemed scientists back then were warning of an imminent ice age. It seems that science can't get its shit together about much of anything. This should be patently obvious by the mad rush to create Artificial Intelligence (along the lines of *The Matrix*) and herd humanity into a scientific wet dream culture of human cyborgs implanted with computer chips to create a new global network of artificial hive intelligence. Sadly, it appears that our younger tech-addicted generations are all stoked up about this possibility, and whatever common sense humanity once may have had is rapidly evaporating. Despite movies and novels reporting the very likely negative outcome of such cavalier abuses of inventiveness (*The Terminator films, The Matrix, The Forbin Project/Colossus, Westworld, etc*), the Silicon Valley crowd and their globalist compatriots are progressing into robotics at breakneck speed as if they have struck gold. The commonsense aspect of 'proceed with caution' is peculiarly absent in this technological arena. Merging humans with machines is not 'evolution', it is a forced adjustment on a species that has become so tech addicted that there is little thought given to the ramifications of such a scenario if it were to play out in actuality.

Within the communist globalist ideology, the concept of the 'useless eaters' has been prevalent for a long time. We are told that with robotics we will all live lives of luxury while robots attend to our every need and desire (sex robots are already being manufactured), which is the lure for humanity to buy into this nightmare techno-scam. If the communist globalist, would-be world controllers have already fabricated two World Wars and the never-ending wars since that time to control the population of useless eaters, what do you think will happen when they have robotic intelligence to take the place of all these useless eaters? It is not hard to envision a scenario of pod people as illustrated in *The Matrix* as but one grim solution. I doubt, however, that the globalists would even resort to creating a wirehead human culture like that except as an interim stage until they could eliminate most of humanity from their global playground of the elite. With this grim scenario I think it is plain to see that this mergence of humans and machines would not beget any real shift in consciousness. It would just be another way to cheapen human existence, and the world controllers already believe that 99% of humanity is disposable cattle as it is, to do with as they will (and have done throughout recorded history).

Understand, I am not averse to technology, but I am highly averse to the abuses to which technology has been applied since the industrial age into the present. Rather than elevating the overall human condition, in most cases technological advances have been used to produce weapons of war and psychological manipulation tools to control the human herds more than anything else.

Within the realm of neuroscience, it wasn't until about 2014 that the word consciousness was even allowed in the scientific community for most of the last century. Consciousness was disparagingly referred to as the 'C' word and was viewed with as much favorability as the 'N' word holds in politically correct speech today. Although the progenitors of psychology were wrapped up in solving the mystery of the *psyche* (soul) through investigating mediums and seeking to understand the difference between life and the alleged afterlife, psychology was co-opted by the materialists and all subjective experiences were ruled out as having any validity. To materialist science, all that mattered was to figure out the mechanics of the brain, which science feels is the driver of the human biocomputer. For more information on this aspect of scientific studies into consciousness I recommend, *Consciousness and the Brain: Deciphering how the Brain Codes our Thoughts* by Stanislas Dehaene (2014).

Because consciousness was a dirty word in the realm of materialist science, over the past century the study of consciousness was left to the speculative realms of philosophers, where it has always been firmly ensconced since the meanderings of Plato and the early Greek and Hindu philosophers seeking to commune with the alleged 'Divine'. I fully exposed and explained all this in depth in *The Truth About the 'Divine' Soul*.

The fact is that no one knows what consciousness is to begin with, which is why we have been plagued with thousands of years of speculative philosophy seeking to figure it out. I can't provide an answer to what consciousness is, only that *it is*. Some things defy explanation and seeking to find answers to the unanswerable only amounts to tail chasing and meaningless hours and years spent on investigating total imponderables. Sometimes we just have to accept that what is *is* and leave it at that. Consciousness is one of those is's. At best we can only vaguely see how it works from the standpoint of subjective experience. Finally, as noted in Dehaene's book, science has recognized that to understand consciousness at all they are finally going to have to pay attention to subjective experiences, which they have discounted for almost a century or more seeking to define consciousness through strictly materialist mechanistic means of brain study and neuroscience.

Rather than seeking to explain what consciousness is, we would be much wiser to understand how it can function to its greatest potential within us. At present, humanity is stone cold ignorant about cognitive advancement and it is usually equated with intelligence and thinking more than with subjective *perceptual awareness*. Even our concepts of awareness and attention operate in a very narrow range of perceptions in the first cognition world. These perceptions are not only filtered by the brain, what it pays attention to and what it filters out, we each have areas of selective blindness based on our beliefs and personal experiences that create even stronger cognitive and emotional filters. In essence, we are dealing with the unconscious filters of the brain overlaid with conscious filters of beliefs and our perceptions about them, along with more hidden subconscious emotional filters based on our experiences. Dehaene's book discusses the aspects of attention and how the brain filters and processes information both consciously and unconsciously. The focus in this chapter has less to do with the biomechanics of the brain and more to do with our waking state or conscious system of filtering information for acceptance or denial.

Regardless of the basis for the belief in a shift in consciousness, such a change is on the immediate horizon, and this will be discussed in depth in my next book, *Explaining the Shift in Consciousness: Translating the 'Becoming' Book from the New Paradigm Trilogy*. The bad part about most of the current beliefs about this shift in consciousness is that it will be magically painless, and people will just shift consciousness like turning a page in a book or changing clothes. It is not going to be that simple or painless. We have seen one example in *The Matrix* film when Neo had to come face to face with the truth about the Matrix.

Another film that provides a message about the coming shift in consciousness is with the *Stargate SG1* post-series film, *The Ark of Truth*, which I will summarize briefly below.

In the film there is a group of organized religious zealots called the Ori who are seeking to conquer the galaxy. They preach the religion of Origin, which is a religion of Ascended Masters who cannot interfere with lesser developed human species (much like the truth I have revealed about Ninhursag and the hive). To circumvent this non-intervention rule between the Ascended Masters and humans, they create ranks of what they call Priors to serve as their intermediaries to convince and coerce undeveloped humans to worship the Ascended Masters as gods (no different than the reality I've revealed in my own works).

There was allegedly a race of 'good guys' referred to throughout the *SG1* series episodes who also 'ascended' and are referred to as the Ancients. Before these ancient humans ascended, they had already been at war with the other Ascended Masters who created the Ori. As such, they created a secret weapon called the Ark of Truth that, once opened, would show the Ori Priors the error of their ways in worshipping the Ascended Masters as gods. Spoiler alert. At the end of the film, the Ark of Truth is opened, and all the Ori Priors get their massive 'oh shit' moment of realization of the truth and repent their ways, crying because 'they didn't know', etc. This shift in consciousness portrayed in this science fiction film is a very close approximation of how the shift in consciousness is going to occur when it does, except it is not going to be selective to one group of people. It is going to spread across the multiverse and all other creations in virtually an instant and everyone is going to be faced with the fallacy of every belief they harbored in an instant, both about themselves as well as the external first cognition world of illusion.

The processes we have shared about internal housecleaning and cell talk and altering mindsets have all been in preparation for those who can do so, to sort of immunize themselves from the harshest effects when this shift in consciousness occurs. The more personal belief garbage you shed, the better prepared you will be to ride out the shift when it happens. For everyone else, it is going to be a very unpleasant ride and the chances are that many won't survive it. The reader can take this information as presented or leave it. It is up to your discretion. More explanations about this shift will be forthcoming in *Explaining the Shift in Consciousness* book.

18. Into the Hinterlands

As I noted in *Navigating into the Second Cognition* using the analogy of an hourglass, the further one progresses into the hinterlands of second cognition understanding, the more acutely one perceives. People have asked me how it is that I can present the earth-shattering material I do in my books, how is it that I can perceive what I do to write these exposés. The advancement in perceptual capabilities, once one crosses that second cognition threshold, are incalculable in their immensity. It is a continuing upward spiral to perceptions and awareness that we are only now starting to scratch the surface of. Even with all I know and presently perceive, I know I don't know shit compared to what can be known in the long run, even in this human lifetime.

I have elucidated many psychological observations in this volume as I have in a number of prior works. Psychologists can tell you what they observe about how humans function with these psychological habits, but they can't tell you *why* these habits function as they do with the sameness they do across the spectrum of humanity. It takes advanced perceptions to see through to the root causes of these symptoms to explain them to others. Observing and identifying psychological habits does not explain *why* they occur, only that they are observable. It takes greater perceptual awareness to see through to solving the mystery of the *why*.

Although the material in this book is explained as well as I can for first cognition cognitive digestion, it doesn't mean that all readers are really going to *see* it beyond the conceptual and intellectual basis. One's ability to *see* through the illusion to the reality, to find the why's in the midst of the what's and how's, is what second cognition advanced perceptual awareness brings you. This book would not have been possible without my own continuing advancement into the hinterlands of second cognition understanding, and I know there is more to come. If any of you have wondered how I perceive what to write and how I do it, it is all due to an active collaboration with the psoyca sentience that resides within this human form. I have chosen to fully collaborate with this sentient awareness, and I see exquisitely how it is benefitting my life in this human form. The same option is there for anyone else to pursue if they can only stay the course and not give up on themselves in this grueling process of personal growth.

The doorway to the second cognition awaits all who work to get there. The unknown and immeasurable hinterlands that lie beyond that doorway will provide unlimited cognitive advancement and creativity for all who actively choose to venture there. Without some personal motivation to get there in some capacity, even the shift in consciousness will not push you through that doorway.

Our books provide the roadmap, not only for reaching the second cognition doorway, but for what that doorway can open up to any of you. The multiverse is vast in its expanses and we have yet to discover the inner workings of our human minds and bodies. The latter is the first rung on the ladder to reaching for the stars.

I have done my best in this volume to give you more tools to do your own inner housecleaning with and explain as best I can what it is you are shooting for, and in part, what to anticipate as you move yourself toward the second cognition state of awareness. It is all about pragmatism and sobriety, not mysticism and faux spirituality.

As the old adage goes, "Know thyself". That is your pathway to cognitive freedom and opening the doorway to infinity. Rid yourself of the virus tyrant programs operating within you, and every one you remove puts you that much closer to knowing who and what you really are, as well as what you can become. I wish you the best on your journey.

The Evolution of Consciousness Series

Book 1

A Philosophy for the Average Man: An Uncommon Solution to a World Without Common Sense by Endall Beall

Book 2

Willful Evolution: The Path to Advanced Cognitive Awareness and a Personal Shift in Consciousness by Endall Beall

Book 3

Demystifying the Mystical: Exposing Myths of the Mystical and the Supernatural by Providing Solutions to the Spirit Path and Human Evolution by Endall Beall

Book 4

Navigating into the Second Cognition: The Map for your journey into higher Conscious Awareness by Endall Beall

Book 5

The Energy Experience: Energy work for the Second Cognition by Mrs. Endall Beall

Book 6

We Are Not Alone – Part 1: Advancing Cognitive Awareness in an Interactive Universe by Endall Beall

Book 7

We Are Not Alone – Part 2: Advancing Cognitive Awareness through Historical Revelations - Endall Beall

Book 8

Advanced Teachings for the Second Cognition by Mrs. Endall Beall

Book 9

We Are Not Alone – Part 3: The Luciferian Agenda of the Mother Goddess by Endall Beall

Companion Volumes to The Evolution of Consciousness Series

False Prophecies, Reassessing Buddha and the Call to the Second Cognition by Endall Beall

Operator's Manual for the True Spirit Warrior by Endall Beall

Spiritual Pragmatism: A Practical Approach to Spirit Work in a World Controlled by Ego by Endall Beall

Revamping Psychology: A Critique of Transpersonal Psychology Viewed From the Second Cognition by Endall Beall & Mrs. Endall Beall

The Common Sense Revolution: Creating Common Ground and Genuine Common Sense – Endall Beall and the Psoyca Crew (2016)

Second Cognition Series

Book 1

The New Paradigm Transcripts: Teachings for a New Tomorrow by Endall Beall & Doug Michael

Book 2

Breaking the Chains of the First Cognition: Tools for Understanding the Path to the Second Cognition by Endall Beall & Doug Michael

Book 3

PSOYCA – Road to the Second Cognition by Endall Beall & Doug Michael

Book 4

The Energetic War Against Humanity: The 6,000 Year War Against Human Cognitive Advancement by Endall Beall

Book 5

The Cognitive Illusion of History: How Humanity Has Been Controlled Through Selective and Biased Historical Reporting by Endall Beall & Doug Michael

Book 6

The Second Cognition Toolbox: Requirements for Advancing Your Consciousness by Endall Beall

Book 7

Firestarters: The Gemma and Endall Transcripts – by Endall Beall and Gemma Beall

Book 8

No Trespassing: Creating a New World Based on Mutual Respect by Endall Beall

Book 9

Psoyca Consciousness by Endall Beall

Companion Volumes to the Second Cognition Series

Understanding Wisdom: A Treatise on Wisdom Viewed from the Second Cognition by Endall Beall

From Belief to Truth – From Truth to Wisdom by Endall Beall

The Psychology of Becoming Human: Evolving Beyond Psychological Conditioning by Endall Beall

Standalone Work: Available for free .pdf download at our website

Clarifying the don Juan Teachings for the Second Cognition: A Pragmatic Reanalysis Without the Mystical Misdirection – by Endall Beall

Beyond Don Juan: Into the Third Attention – The Second Cognition (2019) by Endall Beall

Find free pdf downloads for these books at the links below, or look for them under the header of Companion Books to the Series at our website below

Beyond Second Cognition Series

Book 1

Gutting Mysticism: Explaining the Roots of All Supernatural Belief by Endall Beall (2018) by Endall Beall

Book 2

Religion, the Goddess and the Mind Virus of Heaven: The Deception of Holiness in Human Belief Systems (2018) by Endall Beall

Book 3

Introduction to the Multiverse: The Layman's Guide to the Cosmos (2018) by Endall Beall

Book 4

Facing the Truth: Conspiracy or Plan? 100 Years of Subversive Psychological Warfare Against America (2018) by Endall Beall

Book 5 – *The No Rules Multiverse: The Endeavor to Repair a Faulty Creation (2019) – Endall Beall*

Book 6 – *Into the Hinterlands: Beyond Second Cognition (2019) by Endall Beall*

Companion Volumes to Beyond Second Cognition Series

Emotionalism: How the Human Herds are Controlled (2019) by Endall Beall

The Truth About the 'Divine' Soul: The Late Creation of the Concept of Heaven (2019) by Endall Beall

Challenging Philosophy and the Philosophers" Explaining Nietzsche to Philosophical Academia (2019) – Endall Beall

Upcoming Volumes

Explaining the Shift in Consciousness: Translating the 'Becoming' book from the New Paradigm Trilogy by Endall Beall

Mission Earth: Advanced Messages for Psoyca Ground Crew by Endall Beall

The Flesh Robot: The Truth About the Human Computer by Gemma Beall and Endall Beall

For questions or inquiries contact the authors at *http://demystifyingthemystical.com/#/*

Further work by these authors can be found at the Gemma Beall YouTube channel at
https://www.youtube.com/channel/UCN3VfiNrozRSUBiDIR8k9EA

Or through the Gemma Beall Patreon channel for subscriptions of $5 per month for access to 300 video presentation, and $7 per month for all the videos and an expanding number of educational podcasts, chapter previews, blogs and an interactive comment forum.
https://www.patreon.com/GemmaBeall/

www.ingramcontent.com/pod-product-compliance
Lightning Source LLC
Chambersburg PA
CBHW061749250726
48657CB00001B/54